ADVANCE PRAISE FOR
BORN TO SHINE

"This book will change your life. Do you feel like you're stuck? Or maybe like you're just going through the motions? Ashley LeMieux will grab you by the hand and guide you to your truth. Never has a book capturing such despair and heartbreak been so inspirational and motivational. The powerful beam of light that shines from this author will truly illuminate the way for every reader, and when you've reached the final page you too will feel ready to take your first huge step toward reclaiming your life and your light."

>   -**Mallory Ervin**, Online Thought Leader, Podcaster

"Ashley is a shining example of turning absolutely devastating loss into something purposeful and beautiful. She will inspire so many in the midst of their deep suffering to find the healing and hope within themselves, to turn their painful wounds, traumas and hurts into sacred scars."

>   -**Ruthie Lindsey**, Speaker, Author

"A story of courage, hope, and healing that will remind you that life is tough, but so are you. Ashley opens herself up to the heartbreak and healing in a way that causes you to reflect on your own life and your own journey with pain and hope. *Born to Shine* instills in us the belief that we can make it through the hard seasons of life and in those darkest seasons, we can be a light to the world that is so desperately needed. Our stories matter and this story is proof that grief and healing can share space, can co-exist while we figure out how to navigate the harder chapters of our lives."

-**Jenna Kutcher**, Top Online Influencer, Top Podcaster

"Few people can achieve the balance of delivering a raw and personal story in a way that is relevant, applicable, and powerful to someone with a completely different story. Ashley has done that so beautifully in *Born to Shine*. This a tool, not just for the woman who desperately need to experience healing but also for any gal who needs to learn how to live beyond her circumstances with boldness, joy, and confidence."

-**Jordan Dooley**, Best Selling Author

"While the causes may be different, there isn't a human alive who gets through this life without being challenged by heartbreak or adversity. Ashley LeMieux has been in the depths of despair, and fought her way back becoming one of the most inspiring and positive people I know. Born to Shine teaches us when all is lost, how to find hope."

-**Sara Walsh**, Emmy Award Winning Sportscaster

"The way Ashley tells her story, but also invites me to examine my own story, my own trials, my own life—is both masterful and powerful. I was moved by the unique exercises she offers for self-reflection and found new insight and beauty into my own life. Through Ashley bravely sharing her heart, I was able to see new facets of my own."

-**Alison Faulkner**, Speaker and founder of The Alison Show

BORN TO SHINE

Born to Shine

PRACTICAL TOOLS TO HELP YOU SHINE, EVEN IN LIFE'S DARKEST MOMENTS

Ashley LeMieux

NEW YORK

LONDON • NASHVILLE • MELBOURNE • VANCOUVER

BORN TO SHINE

Practical Tools to Help You SHINE, Even in Life's Darkest Moments

Published in New York, New York, by Morgan James Publishing. Morgan James is a trademark of Morgan James, LLC. www.MorganJamesPublishing.com

ISBN 9781642793840 paperback
ISBN 9781642793857 eBook
Library of Congress Control Number: 2018914173

Cover Design by:
Meredith Carty
mercarty.com &
Chris Treccani
www.3dogcreative.net

Interior Design by:
Christopher Kirk
www.GFSstudio.com

Morgan James is a proud partner of Habitat for Humanity Peninsula and Greater Williamsburg. Partners in building since 2006.

Get involved today! Visit
MorganJamesPublishing.com/giving-back

CONTENTS

Part Four: Your Light is Constant

For Mike, Z, and S.
Thank you for teaching me how to shine in the darkest night.
I love you to the moon and back.
Forever.

Introduction:
FINDING YOUR LIGHT

March 5, 2017

    "Today I deflated; I gave up. How in the world could a human possibly feel so incapable of doing something so good and still be expected to take another step forward? I had given it my all and was sure it was going to work out, but it didn't. What a total failure I was. What a waste. This is how they feel—the people who stop dreaming, who get stuck, who lose faith in themselves, in each other, and in God. What do I do now? What do I give when I have nothing left inside of me? This is how they feel. I'm not supposed to feel this way. They are."

There is no *they*, there is only *us*. All of us, all 7.4 billion inhabitants of planet Earth suffer, but why does our unique and personal pain always feel so isolating? Why, in our sorrow, does it feel impossible to breathe, when all around us people seem to be thriving in the midst of their own struggles?

In 2013, my husband, Mike, and I became parents overnight. We signed on to become the permanent legal guardians to S and Z, two wonderful, magical children we loved with all of our hearts and with every last speck of our beings. S and Z called us "Mom and

Dad." They took our last name. We said our prayers together and dreamed about the future we would share. Four short years later though, after Mike and I pursued formal adoption, S and Z were returned to their biological family. I never got to kiss them goodbye.

I wrote the above journal entry in my new house, at an empty kitchen table sitting more than a thousand miles away from the place where it all happened, the place I grew up, the place where I raised my children and thought I would one day help them their raise theirs. I was trying to find my footing again, trying to learn who I was without them. It was something I thought I once knew, but when my children were taken, they took a huge chunk of me with them. The strong, wide-eyed, and full-of- faith girl I used to be was less than a shadow; she was a chalk outline on the ground. For the next year, inhaling and exhaling felt like work. Life seemed so easy for everybody else, but all I could see when I woke up and looked outside, even on the brightest day, was darkness.

The loss of the deep love Mike and I had been gifted with so briefly weighed on me, but one day while washing my face, it hit me: I could not simply sit back and watch myself slog through this grief. The only person I could nudge and watch thrive was myself. If I wanted to see the light, I was going to have to *be* the light. I was going to have to stop looking outward and begin looking in. I was going to have to participate in living.

I have learned, not just through our difficult adoption experience, but through a series of hard experiences, to stop trying to prove my worth. The value of each human life is immeasurable. The light that shines within me does not rely on one moment, or one effort; it does not hinge upon one failure or one success. My light is constant and unchanging, and there is something intrinsically wonderful about me that cannot be stripped away, calculated, or reproduced by anything or anybody else.

To make this determination, I had to travel into and out of some low dark places where I hated myself, where I couldn't see myself. In these places, my light was nothing but a flicker. But through a conscious process of self-discovery, I traveled upwards. From the grandest summits of life, I could see my light was absolutely everywhere. Joy reflected off of joy and everything felt perfect. On my journey through the peaks, the plateaus, the valleys, and the canyons, in meeting my children and in losing them, I learned that my light—my ability to generate love and absorb it, to shine—is a powerful tool. With it, even in my bleakest moment, there is hope.

Seeing your light, knowing it is there even when it is only a flicker, means that in the dark places, you don't have to be afraid anymore. If this can be true for me, it can be true for YOU.

Within these pages, it is my hope you will come to claim your light, rejoice in it, and take comfort in the knowledge it is always there, even when your life is in ruins. Especially in those gloomy, shadowy places, you may discover you shine your brightest. In living through stories with me about what it means to shine, I hope you grow to understand:

- *Your light is yours.* Because your light is born in you and sustained in you, you have nothing to prove to anyone else. You hold the match and the bucket of water, and both always and only belong to you.
- *Your light is contagious.* When you shine, you are a beacon to those in the dark. Relish in what it means to help light another's path. Walk beside your sister, hear her story, share your own, remind her of the beautiful, sacred glow she has inside when she feels she has lost it. Realize and reaffirm the light does feel lost sometimes, for all of us.
- *Your light will get heavy.* When you can't pay your rent, or your car is broken, or somebody you love is gone, it's

easy to set down the torch and walk away. It will be work to keep your light going some days, but it will be good work. It's okay too for the work to be hard, or to feel bad at it some days. When our demons are ready to be on their way, they don't always present us with perfectly wrapped packages of understanding and personal growth (in fact, some of our demons never seem to leave us at all). But it is okay to heal imperfectly and for our wounds to be become scars. We all carry baggage, but we can carry light at the same time. The balance is absolutely worth struggling for.

- *Your light is constant.* No matter how many of your dreams, hopes, and goals have slipped away, YOU are still shining. The light ebbs and flows, flickers and flashes, but it is always there, shining in you. The fact that life can be dark, unfair, and full of sorrow and grief does not diminish your capacity for light, love, and goodness.

Wherever you are in your life right now, give yourself permission to be there. Accept yourself as you are. Feel the weight, the joy, and the sadness of whatever circumstances surround you and know your story is not over yet. Life has changed, life will continue to change, but your infinite value will not, no matter what. You will still be shining, even as you weep.

I'm no scientist or guru, but I hope by sharing my very human story, I will help you see the beauty in yours. As you see me uncover and reclaim my light, I hope you will find comfort and solace in yours. The path I took is laid out in these pages, and though your path might look different, I hope you'll find the courage to begin or continue along your unique journey. These stories are sacred and special—as are yours. Feelings of loss and brokenness caused by pain and grief are some of the darkest places we may dwell, but here we learn the most about light. Where we struggle to catch a ray of hope, we learn we are born to shine.

Part One:

YOUR LIGHT IS YOURS

Chapter One:
SOMEBODY LOVES YOU

Somebody loves you. It's as simple and as powerful as that. I'm not talking about the sophomoric "crush-slipping-you-a-note-and-a-gaze-full-of-hormones-in-the-hall" kind of love, I'm talking about the big love, the baffling, philosophical soul-glue that holds us all together. Somebody out there really, deeply, truly, loves YOU, and guess what? They're doing it right now in this pristine little moment. How incredible is that?!

Love is great for poetry, but like most invisible, immeasurable things, it isn't especially easy to define, it's the mystery that's haunted us, tortured us, and thrilled us, since the very beginning of time, and it means a thousand different things to a thousand different people. I'm no Plato, but I might as well join the great thinkers and take a crack at it. To me, love is the origin of humanity, it's what makes us *us*, different from the rest of the birds and bees and little brown bears. Love is the magic that got us here and it's the magnetic force that keeps us connected. I was connected from day one.

I was a chubby baby, not much hair, plenty of knee fat, and like most new arrivals, I loved love right from the get-go. I loved love so much that I made my poor parents delirious and miserable. They couldn't put me down, not to drink a water or go to the bathroom, they had to hold me all of the time or else I'd scream bloody murder. I'd sleep for ages, like a perfect peaceful cherub, but only if I was cradled snug and warm in their arms. They tried everything: swaddling, lullabies, mobiles. When they thought I was out cold, puffy arms limp, lips making those dreamy baby wiggles, they would try to put me down, but the second my fuzzy head hit the mattress, I would reach out physically (and vocally) for another taste of the good stuff, that undeniable, sustaining love and every time I reached out, it would be there, without fail, to lift me.

Babies have the love stuff figured out. They trust implicitly that when they cry out (or even when they don't), somebody will be along shortly to hold, nurture, and protect them. As we get older, as we start experiencing a little more of the world, love gets a little more complex. Anger, mistrust, broken promises, competition, those terrible middle school years, betrayal, abuse, injustice, inadequacies, and a litany of other heartbreaks start taking their toll. One day, a day that seems like any other, we open our arms, reach out, and nobody arrives to lift us up. We begin to question everything, we stop believing that we *are* loved, and we stop reaching out for it.

I remember the exact day when, for me, love got tricky. In elementary school, I had the honor of taking down the American flag with three other girls once. It was a privilege, the biggest deal for the littlest people. At our school, taking down the flag meant that you were either a good leader or a good listener, and spoiler alert, I was a champion listener, quiet as a mouse and mousy as a mouse, shy and perfectly content in my spot at the very back of the Reading Rug. The girls who were on flag duty with me, were leaders, or at least they were popular, tall, and liked to sit on the "cool" bench between the orange tree and soccer goal and watch the boys play football. We were all far too young to understand why a girl would want to watch a boy do anything at all, but this was their chosen activity. I was never invited to the bench, more often than not, I was out there in the field getting my high tops muddy, tossing the Nerf, and blending in seamlessly with the boys thanks to my knee-length denim shorts and very bad haircut. Flag day was the first time I found myself on the other side. I didn't have a lot of friends, you don't typically when you're quiet and mousy, but deep in my heart, I still wanted them, I still loved love.

As recess neared its end, it was go-time. I approached the girls, let's call them all Stephanie, ready, ready to reach out for friendship, ready to ask for love, and very, very ready to receive it. I was ecstatic, envisioning playdates and swapping juice boxes and bonding over the bubble gum and Barbies I didn't yet own. The Stephanies were sitting on their bench comparing geometric spandex bicycle shorts when I strode up, smiling like a lunatic, unknowingly vulnerable, and reaching out to them as hard as I possibly could.

"Hi there!"

I said it too loud and immediately regretted not saying "'sup?" instead the way the older kids did.

The Stephanies looked up at me for one hopeful moment, but they quickly returned to a heated discussion about what they should collectively wear to the Harvest Festival the next weekend, it was between pink stirrup pants and black ones. I just stood there, staring, in all my mousy glory, invisible pair of arms stretched out towards them, waiting to be embraced.

Stephanie One, who was lobbying for pink pants, silenced the group. She looked right at me and sneered, "How does it feel to be you, Ashley? To have five shirts hanging in your closet that you just rotate through, never having to care about what you're wearing looks like. You have it *so* easy, not having any nice clothes to wear, not having anyone look at you…"

Laughter followed.

Stephanie Two thought this was hilarious, so funny that she swung her vote from black to pink pants just to reward her friend for her unabashed meanness. Stephanie Three shot me a knowing, apologetic glance, like she wanted to be kind, but knew it would result in her expulsion from the coveted bench by the orange tree. She forced out a few, pitiful giggles because back in those days, that's what a person had to do to maintain their rank as the third best Stephanie in school.

I ran my hands down my favorite green shirt trying to hide the ketchup splotch from lunch and smooth the wrinkles that I had walked into school with that morning. It was true, I *did* have just five tee shirts. I hardly ever thought about what I wore or what anyone else did for that matter, I just wanted to be loved and I didn't know that love had such a strict dress code. In that moment, surrounded by three pants-obsessed maybe-friends passing judgment on an actual bench, I was ruled an outcast, my crime was wearing wrinkly tee shirts that were nowhere near pink enough, and I was devastated. The verdict was in, I was officially unlovable.

Rejection—it's just about the most awful feeling in the world, isn't it? It's being left out of the grand, secret club, forgotten, deemed not good enough, passed by like a piece of sidewalk trash. It's the fast working needle full of Novocaine that starts to numbs us to the love we were born to feel. After a few seconds of just standing there, struck dumb by the swift dismissal, I took off running, past the football field, past the flag, straight into the second bathroom stall from the end. I felt subhuman, stupid for just assuming I was worthy of being loved. And by a Stephanie, no less! After all, how could I possibly be loved with the wrong kind of shirt on and bad hair and ketchup obscuring my Nike swoosh?! I plonked down onto the toilet and wiped my eyes with single-ply toilet paper until my cheeks were chapped.

As this sad scene was unfolding in the bathroom, just a few classroom doors down from where I was squatting and crying, something incredible was happening, somebody was busy loving me. My little sister, Brooke, was hunched over a set of watercolors and fat kindergarten paint brushes, adoring me, basking in the light I didn't even know that I had yet. She was making me a rainbow, about fourteen wobbly lines of color that all blended into brownish goo stretched between big blobby clouds. Underneath it, stood two crazy-happy twig people with twelve fingers on each hand, they were sisters, her and I. Now, I loved my sister, but I wasn't always nice to her. I picked everyone else before her during our cul-de-sac kickball games because she wasn't very good, and I always took the cookie with the most chocolate chips. Brooke didn't care though, because she loved me, wrinkly shirts, vicious kickball team management style, and all.

After school, she ran up to me with her giant, crinkly, just-dried painting flapping in the wind, and backpack and pigtails smacking against her bony little shoulders.

"Ashley! Ashley! Look! I made this for you!"

My face was still swollen and sad, but she was glowing (She was also winded. The reasons I picked her last for kickball were very, very real.). Her pink cheeks balled up into a grin, and she handed me the paper.

"Here!"

She was so proud.

Sure enough, under a brownish rainbow was a giant-eyed, many fingered, triangle torso-ed testament to my beloved-ness. Even though we were in the middle of the playground in front of the big kids, the cool kids, and all of the kids inbetween, you better believe I let that little sister of mine hug me. She buried her head into the unsightly tee shirt that everyone hated and we stood there together until our mom honked the horn. She reached out to me, and I welcomed her into my arms. Brooke didn't know it, I probably didn't either, but that day, I was reaching out for her too.

It took a little humiliation and a hideous rainbow, but I learned something that day. I was loved, not just approved of or popular, but really, truly, to-the-bones loved. Brooke wasn't the only one who loved me either. I had parents who cherished me, who let me wear the same five tee shirts over and over again because those were the ones I liked, and who spent the first two years of my life not sleeping so that I could. I had God, the ultimate love, the force that put me here and would always be there to help guide me when I felt uncertain, and I had myself, though my confidence was more than a little shook, I knew that if I was worth reaching out to and making rainbows for, I was worth loving. Sisters, somebody loves me and somebody loves you too—we just forget sometimes.

The shady thing about love is that even when it's there, all around us, it isn't always easy to find. As human beings who grow and change and make mistakes, there's a lot we're tasked with seeing past to get to that beautiful truth. Fear, rejection, trauma, brain chemistry, any number of negative experiences or relationships, can all obscure the great love that exists in the world for us. It doesn't help that the people who love us don't always do it perfectly (Come on, guys! Get it together!). Sometimes they hurt us by accident, sometimes they do it on purpose. Sometimes they love us as much as they are capable of and still, it just doesn't feel like enough. Sometimes, if we're truly honest with ourselves, *we're* the ones who cock the whole thing up, we aren't good wives or neighbors, we settle on love-ish replica feelings born from addictions, self-doubt, alcohol, social media, bad boyfriends, bad girlfriends, food, money, you name it, to avoid reaching out for the real thing. But no matter how hazy your world might look, the truth, the glorious, undeniable truth, is still standing up tall on the other side of the fog—somebody loves *you.*

The Somebody who loves you doesn't care about wrinkled shirts, or how many clothes you have hanging in your closest. The Somebody who loves you doesn't mind that you burned dinner or ran late again for school drop-off, or didn't lose the weight that's been bugging you for a decade. The Somebody who loves you could be a family member, a friend, a child, or a really good dog. Somebody who I *know* loves you is your Creator, the source of your light, divinity, love, power, and goodness. God loves YOU wholly, exactly as you are. And you are whole, because you were created that way, you are adored, cherished, and lovingly made. Somebody else who I very strongly suspect loves you is YOU. You're here reading this book not because you love me, but because you love YOU. You're here because you love yourself enough not just to want different results in your lives, but to seek them. You want your power back, and you deserve it. You want love in abundance; you deserve that too. You want to uncover that glorious light that lives in you, that everyone else seems to see *except* you, and you know what? By reading these first pages and taking these first steps, you've already begun.

Since we don't all have a Brooke who conveniently pops up whenever we're in the middle of an emotional crisis in the bathroom (Trust me, if I could bottle her up and send her to you, I would.), the real, valuable practice here is learning in those moments of insecurity, to remind yourself of that Somebody of yours. Before you read one more page filled with my words, it's your turn to write some of your own.

Whenever I feel one of those nasty, shadowy feelings creep in and I don't have my Brooke handy, I write two lists. The first is *Ten Reasons I Love Myself*. I sit down, take a deep breath, and come up with a whole battery of reasons why I'm worthy of the love I know exists for me. Sometimes, it's easy, it takes just five minutes, I decide that I love my jokes, my nose, and my inability to cook anything at all; sometimes, it feels like there are a hundred things to celebrate about Ashley LeMieux. Other times, though, the list of lovables feels closer to two. No matter how long it takes, how bad a job I do, I sit, stay mindful, and take the time to love on myself. It's your turn now.

Ten Reasons I Love Myself

(Psssssssst! If you're stuck, has anyone ever complimented you on your excellent taste in reading material?)

The next list, *Ten Ways I Will Share Love with Others*, is my actual secret weapon. It helps me set a good intention on a bad day, and it's the quickest way to remind myself that I'm worthy of love simply by my capacity to provide it for others. Get out there and give love, think about those who need it, think about what you can offer to the world, write it down, and make it happen.

Ten Ways I Will Love Others

(Remember, it can be as simple as a brown rainbow.)

Life is filled with love, it's hiding everywhere, in those happy lines at the edges of your smile, in the tenderly written music coming through your radio. There's more of it here than you could possibly know what to do with, but sometimes, you have to sit down and be present with it, really remind yourself that it's there. When you're talking down to yourself, somebody out there is talking you up; when you feel worthless, somebody is out there treasuring you;

when you reach out, somebody is reaching back. Friends, somebody loves you, a whole, awful lot. I know I do.

Chapter Two:
DON'T LET IT STOP YOU

The bases were loaded with two outs. The underdog team was down by one run in the final inning, and of course, everybody, even if only in secret, wanted the underdogs to win. A batter walked up to the plate, a batter who had woken up that morning, brushed her teeth, and hoped for this moment, for the opportunity to win the game. She embraced the opportunity and responsibility. Whatever the outcome, it belonged to her, a single beating heart and a whole lot of nerves. She'd seen this kind of high-tension, heroic set-up before in the movies, so she knew which way the story was supposed to go.

The total sum of all her hopes and effort was about to be calculated. In an instant, she would find out if hours of practice, plus bruised body and private batting coaches, added up to what she had heard they would for most of her life. She tightened her grip around the bat and imagined hitting a home run, confetti falling, and applause. She thought about what she would say when she accepted the MVP award and how it would feel to be carried off the field on the shoulders of people she'd always wanted to love her. In the movie, the dream, the poem, it always goes the right way. Reality can shake out a little differently. Regardless, this batter was ready for what she thought she was getting—the dream—nothing less. This batter was me.

Eight years before this memorable moment in softball there was another, although it wasn't quite as cinematic. I was at my first team tryout, plodding around the diamond in the Arizona heat. I was an awkward, insecure tomboy with a bowl cut who was mistaken for a handsome little boy several times a week. At eight years old, I was painfully shy and never wanted to do anything wrong. I was perpetually worried that despite my best efforts, I would disappoint somebody. My parents wanted to help me soar, and their encouragement landed me in center field with a little leather mitt on my hand. Mom and Dad hoped softball would be my launch pad. The diamond would be a place I could learn from.

Hoping for the same, I stood in the middle of a green field in Phoenix and waited. There seemed to be a lot of waiting in softball, but I liked being outside. The idea of being on a team, hitting a ball, and running around in circles appealed to me. That day long ago, I was thinking about the game instead of paying attention to it, and in an instant, the ball was hit high into the air toward my little patch of turf. When it went completely missing in the desert sun, I panicked.

Where's the ball? Can I catch it? Am I doing this right? Everyone is watching! Maybe if I run fast and pretend to trip it won't look so bad if I miss. Maybe...

SMACK!

Too much thinking, not enough catching. The fly ball tumbled back down to earth, and I caught it, directly in my left eye socket. The impact knocked me to the ground. My parents were watching, the coaches were watching, a bench full of other eight-year-old girls was watching. I stood up, stunned, and brushed myself off. I was ready to try again immediately. When you're eight years old, you understand everybody gets smacked in the face by the ball sometimes, and even if you feel a little embarrassed, your parents still love you. You don't let the failure, the fear, or the "IT," stop you.

I don't remember what happened next, but somehow, through a clerical error or recognition of some value in a little girl who acted a bit tougher than she was, I made the team. Actually, I made The Majors, the best little softball team of them all. I was as shocked as my still-throbbing left cheekbone. My parents were so proud they called all of our relatives to let them know I was the next Ken Griffey Jr.

And so, humbly, I began an almost decade-long tenure on the softball field. I travelled to tournaments, hired private batting coaches, logged thousands of hours of way-too-hot practice before and after school. My love of the game might have been born with a fly ball to the face, but it was born nonetheless, because when an eight-year-old girl gets knocked down, she gets right back up again. She doesn't let the IT, the moment of pain, fear, or shame, stop her from playing the game.

In the next eight years of loving softball, starching uniforms, building friendships, and wondering if I would go to college on a sports scholarship, something changed in me. I learned the glorious weight of becoming a part of something, and I became terrified to lose my place. The counterpoint to all the love and joy showed up: Fear.

When we are children, we get to know fear—fear with a lower-case—pretty well. We sleep in the same room as monsters in our closets, we learn to ride two-wheeled bicycles despite skinned knees, and we survive cruel pop quizzes on long division. When we grow up, we try to distance ourselves from things that scare us. We learn to protect ourselves. We remember what it felt like to lose control on our little bike and eat pavement, but we forget what it was like to sail down the sidewalk with happy pink cheeks and wind in our hair.

That day at bat at age sixteen, fear was just beginning to turn to Fear, but still I was ready to win that game. I came to the plate kicking the dirt and shuffling around the way batters do at the Papago Softball Complex. I would not listen to Fear; I would drown out the IT. My team, the Desert Vista Thunder, sat on the bench expectantly, ready to jump up and carry me Cleopatra-style around the bases. I couldn't let them down. The crowd was on their feet shouting, "Wait for a good pitch! Keep your eye on the ball!"

I couldn't let them down either. My mom, her voice filled with so much love and belief, was shouting, "You can do it, Ashley!" at the top of her lungs.

"But what if I don't?" I wanted to yell back. Letting her down would be the worst of all.

The first pitch came, and I leaned into it with all of my might. As I watched the ball soar to left field, the umpire cried, "FOUL BALL!"

The shouting from my coaches and teammates resumed, my pulse picked up, and again I heard the confident voice behind me say, "You can do it, Ashley!"

"But what if I can't?" I replied silently, again.

I can recall every detail of the next sixty seconds. I watched the next pitch crawl towards me in an eerie, astonishing, slow motion. I swung hard, with the same technique I had been taught to use in my hundreds of hours of practice in the wrinkly, rising desert heat. I felt the contact of bat on ball rattle up through my arms. I heard the hollow *thwack* of cork and leather and wood colliding, and I saw the whites of the opposing team's eyes grow bigger and bigger. In that moment, with the feeling the bat sent through my body, I knew that I, Ashley LeMieux, had singlehandedly just led my team to Defeat. Yep, Defeat with a capital "D."

I ran to first base, watching the ball fly high into the air just above the shortstop's head. But this opponent was in the middle of her moment too, and the look on her face was one of sheer determination. Her hope slowly changed to certainty; my hope was dashed. She caught my hit. She won the game, and I lost it. The inning was over, the season was over, and even though I was only a junior in high school, my softball career ended the second I stepped off of that field when Fear began to weigh more than love and joy combined.

Afraid, I never picked up a bat again. I let this singular moment on the field determine my worth and value, leaving any confidence I had in myself right there at home plate. The devastating disappointment, the shame, the sneers from my teammates, the silence from my coaches, it was all too much. I let IT—Fear—stop me. That crushing afternoon on the greenest ball field in Phoenix wasn't my first failure, and it wouldn't be my last, but it might have taught me more than any of the other strikeouts I have made. I learned how powerful Fear can be, and how long it can take to conquer. Somehow, I had grown from an eight-year-old girl who got back up when she hit the dirt to a young woman who wanted to bury herself in it the second things didn't go her way.

We work so hard at learning, developing, growing, course-correcting, and bettering ourselves, so why is it, after years of hard work, we throw it all away over one particularly tough moment or challenge? Why do we allow defeats to weigh so much more than victories? When did pain get bigger than joy? Fear get louder than love? Our math is off, the scale is broken, we need to recalibrate.

When we are kids running around in our light-up shoes, ball caps, and bike shorts at the Papago Softball Complex, we can accept that our fears exist without letting them own us. We accept that facing our closet monsters and bogeymen is a part of growing up. As little ones, we don't mind that we are imperfect and "in progress," we embrace it. We live it! We hear our moms and dads and friends shouting, "You can do it" over grumbles of little critics in our heads telling ourselves, "No you can't." Most importantly, we know that if the dream doesn't shake out, there will always be another at bat and all we need is the courage to step back up to the plate. We get older and forget it's okay to keep growing, failing, and learning. We forget we are "in progress" and always will be. We keep our eyes locked on the scoreboard, and because of it, we miss most of the game.

Now in my thirties, I am still learning there is plenty of game left. Every courageous decision we make gives us another chance to run the bases. Whatever shape Fear takes in your life, whatever makes you put down the bat or walk away from the game, identify it, write it down on piece of paper, and say it out loud. Need help getting started? This is just a sampling of what Fear has looked like to me:

- Not having enough money to get through college.
- Not having the experience or security to start my own company.
- Not having the patience or certainty to become a mother.
- Not having the time, energy, or heart to write a book.

The biggest Fear for many of us is the paralyzing, utter devastation of striking out. Failure is a certainty, it will happen to all of us at some point, but it should never stop us from trying, from being brave, and from opening ourselves up to the possibility of success, love, or happiness. We don't have to spell fear with a capital F; we choose to.

If you can, if you are ready, always extend grace to yourself and confront IT directly. Pick up the bat and do the things that scare you. I picked up the bat again in college. It was a church softball league, but with my first swing back, I hit a home run.

Chapter Three:

YOU'RE THE ONE

.

B efore I met Mike, the bookshelf in my bedroom was lined with just about every relationship advice book you could think of. My personal favorite was *He's Just Not That into You,* a majorly unsettling collection of advice that confirmed all of my worst fears about dating, it was gifted to me by my own well-meaning mother. When your mom is out buying you books on how to hit it big on the dating scene, you can go ahead and assume that you're not doing a terribly good job out there on your own.

I didn't know where exactly I was going wrong, but nothing and nobody seemed to stick. I wasn't boy crazy, and it's not like I had *awful* taste in guys (well, not always), I just wanted someone to fall for me, really, really badly. Instead, though, *I* was the one falling, most times, flat on my face. After a little soul searching and a lot of reading, I began to suspect that the problems I had with love had less to do with the way my boyfriends were treating me and more to do with the way I was treating myself. You can only accept as much love as you feel comfortable receiving and at twenty-years-old, I wasn't comfortable receiving very much at all, especially from *me.*

Somewhere between being banished from a lot of metaphorical and literal benches by a lot of Stephanies throughout my adolescence (If your name is Stephanie, I love you so much! There were just an awful lot of you roaming the desert in the late '90s) and feeling the weight of a society that placed a heck of a lot more value on the outside of a woman than the inside, I'd developed a tendency to seek affection and validation from all of the wrong places. If I was told I was pretty, asked out on a date, or caught a respectable number of eyes on the street, my self-confidence soared, I got a big, old rush of adrenaline that I never wanted to let go of. I liked the thrill of it all so much that I began concentrating on my outsides, just like everybody else was. I went for broke, buying nicer clothes, flat ironing my hair, and applying a self-tanner that smelled like oranges and paint thinner. I was polishing, polishing, polishing, all the while neglecting the parts of myself that really needed the tune-up. I wanted a boy to fall deeply in love with me, and I thought the only way to get there was by looking good in my jeans.

Relationships came and went, and by my late teens, I began to notice some mighty troubling patterns emerging. I would date people that I had nothing in common with because they made me feel pretty, I found myself becoming competitive with other girls and a little bit vain. I was shellacked from head-to-toe, but I felt worse, less like myself than ever. I knew I was really in trouble when I got angry at a boy I dated for not taking me to the ballet and not doing the dishes (and yes, I realized about halfway through my tirade that I was quoting Jennifer Aniston in *The Break Up* verbatim), he just looked at me, offended, and said, "How am I supposed to know what you need? It's not like we ever talk about that stuff!"

He was absolutely right.

After that scene ended, I stomped out of the room, *and* the relationship, and I made a big decision. It was time for a break—not just a dating a break—I needed to take time for some real reflection, a deep dive into the truths about life, myself, and God. I said goodbye to my mountain of hair product and fake tan and went on a mission for my church. It changed everything, I loved the heck out of strangers, felt pure love in return, and for the first time, truly saw and felt my worth. My value wasn't tied up in what boy was interested in me, or how I looked, or what grade I got on a test. It came from a divine sense of purpose and a devotion to serve. I felt more beautiful when I looked in the mirror there with dirt in my teeth and a pink, blistery sunburn, than I ever had before. I was ready for love, the real stuff.

When I got home from the back country in the south, over eighteen months later, I met a wonderful gentleman named Michael LeMieux. Unfortunately for both of us, I don't really remember it at all. He did not sweep me off my feet. We did not lock eyes across a crowded room and see our future in each other's pupils. The whole encounter was about as soul-stirring as shaking your doctor's hand. Mike had seen a photo of me on a mutual friend's desk at work when I was away on my mission, and he was smitten. I was making a silly, gigantic grin in the photo and he couldn't shake the feeling that we were supposed to be together. My friend tried to let him down easy when he asked about me; she told him I was a billion miles away and not interested in dating anybody, but he refused to let me go. Instead of moving on to the next bubbly blonde optimist, he dated that picture of me on the desk for about a year. The day after my plane landed, he invited himself to come out with us.

It was a big group of friends that night, and we were going salsa dancing. In retrospect, salsa dancing was a rather bold outing for a nervous guy to tag along on, but Mike didn't care because he'd been waiting for me. He was so excited he could practically smell the fireworks between us, he caught himself whistling *Lady in Red* reflexively as he got ready, and he plotted out exactly what he was going to say to me. Sadly, across town, I was none the wiser, jumping into a not-red dress and feeling excited to catch up and dance with my dearest, oldest friends. Dating was not on my radar, and neither was he. I walked into the club, gave him a smile and a split-second hand squeeze, and went off to shake it with my girls. That was it.

He didn't lose heart though; I know now that he rarely does. Over the next couple of months, he tagged along on our outings nearly every chance he got. He tried to ask me out to the Arizona State Fair but it didn't even register to me that it was a date because all of our friends ended up piling into the car with us and gabbing so loudly he could hardly get a word in. Again, he was undeterred. Slowly, tenderly, and clumsily, we became friends. We spent more and more time together, and I began to see how different he was than any other guy I had met. He didn't care what I was wearing, or if I had make-up on, he just wanted to talk to me. He'd call at the end of every day just to check in and he'd ask me questions about what I wanted to do in life, where I wanted to travel, if I liked kids. He was the first guy to ever call me "goofy," and I had no idea how to take it. I had no idea how to take *any* of it. A few months in, I finally got the very clearly written memo—Mike liked me, and I liked him too. It seemed impossible, he never talked about how I looked, he didn't play any confusing games, he was kind and sincere, and he treated me well. It just couldn't be! We spent every waking moment together and after three weeks of dating, I stopped looking over my shoulder for the hidden cameras. This was what I'd been waiting for.

Just before Thanksgiving, Mike broke up with me. I was completely caught off guard. Earlier that very day, he'd driven thirty minutes in the wrong direction to leave a handwritten note under my windshield wiper. "Can't wait to see you!" was all it said. That night, as we sat on a bench in the middle of the bridge that crossed Tempe Town Lake, he told me he wanted to *talk*. He was sweaty and started fumbling over his words. I got rattled and felt my lips start to shake. All I could hear was that he wanted to slow things down, he'd never had a serious girlfriend before and was worried things were moving too fast. He kept talking, but I stopped listening to him.

All I could hear was this:

You knew this would happen.

Why would he want you?

You're not pretty enough.

The dialogue wasn't new. It was the same old, post-heartbreak speech I'd been giving to myself quietly for years. Mike and I got up from the bench and walked off. It felt strange to not be holding his hand, but all I wanted was to get to the car, go home, and disappear as quickly as possible. My birthday was in two days and he was supposed to meet my family, I'd have to call them, again, and tell them to buy one less steak for one less boyfriend, again. It was as though nothing had changed at all.

The next day, Mike kept calling and sending me texts that I tried very hard to ignore. I stomped around the house hopped up on hormones and heartache, telling my mom that I wasn't going to do the "one-foot-in-the-door-one-out" relationship, not anymore! No ma'am! Mike could either have all of me, or none of me. My mom just hugged me and smiled at me and probably began planning a trip to Barnes & Noble to pick up another encyclopedic book of love hacks.

Our break up lasted one day. He called and asked me to come over to his house so we could talk in person. He said it was really important, and I missed him terribly, so I agreed. When I showed up, he put his arms around me, he led me up into his room and we stood, just the two of us, in front of his smudgy full-length mirror. He grabbed my hand and said, "This. This is exactly what I want the rest of my life to look like. Ashley, you are exactly who I want to be holding my hand through the rest of my life."

It turns out that Mike hadn't been trying to break up with me at all. He was trying to tell me that the feelings he had for me were big and serious and scary. Instead of listening to him, instead of believing that this incredible person, this love, could be for me, I ran away. I almost lost the love of my life because I didn't let myself believe in it.

We got engaged shortly after that, and I had to keep myself in check. I knew that it in order for Mike to love me fully, the way he wanted to, I was going to have to learn how to love *myself*, be a good partner to *myself*, and believe in *myself*. If I couldn't trust in myself, how could I expect him to trust in me? If I wasn't in touch with my own needs, how could I expect him to meet them? If I wasn't good to me, I wasn't going to be good to us. Practicing self-love is a skill, not just important for relationships, but essential to them.

Our wedding day came around with a flurry of activity, with bunches of flowers and nerves and relatives and excitement. Before I walked down the aisle and made vows and promises to my Mike, my future husband, I found a quiet moment, a full-length mirror just like the one he and I stood before in his room five months earlier, and I made some commitments to myself:

I do promise to honor my needs.

I do promise to be kind to my body.

I do promise to forgive myself.

I do promise to trust in God.

I do promise to believe in myself.

My mom came to get me from the bridal suite. She kissed me on the cheek, fixed my dress, and smiled, relieved, I'm sure, that she wouldn't need to make that trip to Barnes & Noble after all. I walked between the pews of a very full church and not only gave my heart to Mike, but allowed myself confidently, to receive his.

Sisters, I want you to go stand in front of a mirror. I don't care if you haven't showered for a few days, or have sweats on, or if your bathroom looks and smells like a petting zoo. Humor me, go stand in front of your mirror. This won't take long, I swear. Now, I want you to make five promises to yourself. I'm not going to tell you what they should be because you already know, don't you? You've probably known for a long time. Whatever your vows may be, let them be as sacrosanct and serious as the ones you would make to your partner. Take on the responsibility, the privilege, the joy of loving yourself and never settle for less. It won't be easy, marriage isn't either, but it will be worth it, one thousand percent.

We're taught to grow up and find "The One" but girl, you *are* the one, and you need to be before anyone else can share the honor. Whether you're single, married, remarried, divorced, or somewhere in between, you already have the best company life could give you. You have that glorious girl in the mirror. She deserves a lifetime of love and happiness, so let's give it to her.

Chapter Four:

WELCOME TO THE CLUB

W e were young and poor, so we pooled our wedding money and made a down payment on a short-sale condo in Phoenix we got practically for free. The place wasn't our dream house, but it was what we could afford as new-lywed juniors in college needing a home-buyer credit to pay for school. Yep, I told you we were broke kids.

The smell of the downstairs neighbor's weed constantly drifted into our condo. She was always on her front porch taking a smoke break in her pajamas or yelling at people for driving by too fast. Her PJs showed off her calf tattoos perfectly. I liked the cobra on her left leg best, but Mike preferred the Tweety Bird on her right. A few times, I had to call the cops because of illegal activity in the complex. I never called in on our downstairs neighbor, but I did call in about shady-looking deals, and sometimes there would be a burglary or a brawl to spice things up.

One afternoon, not long after Mike and I settled in, we heard a heavy loud banging noise. Our walls were shaking so hard I thought they were going to crumble. The police showed up and explained that the downstairs neighbor's enraged boyfriend had punched holes in the stucco on the exterior of the building. A person could punch through stucco? The petty crime in our little neighborhood was constant. A few nights after the stucco incident, people were busted for selling drugs by the pool. A week after that, there was an all-out 2 A.M. boxing match underneath our window. I peeked through the blinds and watched a few minutes of the bout before calling the cops and whispering to the operator that if anybody asked, the residents of 533 were not, I repeat, *we were NOT* the snitch. The sound of sirens blaring through the Arizona night became strangely comforting, and I vowed to myself every single day that I would work as much as they'd let me at my stressful car dealership job if it meant that we could have a better life. Sadly, the condo wasn't the only thing keeping us from living the dream.

If the home situation was bad, the car situation was worse. I drove an Acura whose new car smell had worn out long ago. She was a hand-me-down vehicle; she'd been my mom's first, then my brother's, and then mine. This car had history and moxie and felt so much like home. I loved her. Unfortunately, this love didn't translate into her working very well, and her quirks made our already imperfect lives decidedly less perfect. In the middle of a Phoenix summer, her windows would get stuck rolled down, so I'd either show up wherever I was going beet red, sweaty, and rocking a 115-degree highway blow-out, or soaking wet after a monsoon. Nobody tells you about the wild, rainy desert monsoons and that if you don't roll your windows up, you should consider wearing a life vest.

The Acura was an embarrassment. When I pulled into my uncle's car dealership before work in the mornings, the mechanics would shake their heads, the ladies in administration would furrow their brows, and the early customers would gasp. Driving a giant blow dryer was no fun, but poor Mike, he was driving an octopus. His sad car guzzled oil and leaked so badly, he left a black, inky trail wherever he went. Eventually, his octopus broke down completely and though neither of us could understand why, my blow dryer got stolen on a Thursday in the middle of the afternoon outside of Mike's work. He had borrowed it because the octopus could no longer handle the 10-mile commute.

At first, Mike and I laughed about our misfortune. Eventually though, we grew tired of the broken things, our crummy condo, our dismal credit scores, and even our bushy-tailed newlywed hearts. We knew we couldn't afford to fix two busted cars, so when mine got swiped we hoped for a sweet insurance pay out. We kept our fingers crossed that the Acura would stay stolen for thirty days so we could buy a used Ford Fusion or Neon, something with windows that rolled all the way up. Auto-theft seemed like the most perfect, weird answer to our prayers, but fourteen days in, the police called and our dream of new used wheels died. My car was waiting for me in the middle of desert, stripped of everything, but still somehow chugging to life. I got her back more damaged than I ever imagined a car could be, but the insurance company refused to declare her totaled. So, we welcomed our battered vehicle back to her spot by the curb, and I hit the road again.

Desert life had not been kind to the blow dryer. The people who borrowed her stole everything from the little stereo to the spare change in the cup holder. They even took the glass cake stand, which had been sitting in the trunk for months since our wedding. Cupboard space was limited in our new condo, and Mike and I weren't exactly looking for a place to display a collection of gourmet éclairs and croissants. We were on more of a Pop Tart budget.

The first time I got back in the driver's seat and turned the key, I immediately knew something was wrong with the engine. The scary yellow "something's-about-to-explode" light, the only light that still worked, stayed on all of the time. Also, no matter how hard I leaned on the gas pedal, my old girl couldn't drive faster than forty miles an hour. Mike was worried about me getting to work safely and begged me to take her in, but we crunched the numbers and there was no way we could afford repairs. This was it, this was where we were in life—our two cars parked outside of a stucco building with holes in it were together worth less than a pair of designer jeans. Driving was humiliating and frustrating. Life was humiliating and frustrating. I started to break down worse than our cars did.

Every morning, I drove my dangerous lemon along the freeway within a sea of actual new cars. People honked incessantly at me, yelling and hollering "What's wrong with you?!" out their perfectly functioning windows, flipping me off as if that would somehow make me drive faster instead of more furious. Even though I stuck to the slow lane—where it's my Arizona Department of Transportation given right to putter along—other drivers were rude, rowdy, and mean. I huffed and puffed and glared back at them; I cussed quietly and shook my fist. After a few commutes, I realized that I wasn't seeing the best in people, and I wasn't seeing the best in myself either. I began to think less about what was going wrong in my life and more about what must be going wrong in theirs. Maybe the people who had those nice air-conditioned automobiles weren't so happy after all? I decided that my Acura and I had better start ignoring the shiny, angry people before we became them. Once I stopped fixating on what I didn't have, a whole new vibrant world opened up to me on the freeway.

One very hot day, running late for my Spanish final, I got stuck behind a car miraculously even slower than mine. I tapped on my brake and cruised up behind the little beater, thrilled and enthralled by the fact that there was somebody else out there who dared to travel Interstate 10 going under forty miles per hour. In a tiny, patched-up Ford that they had given up manufacturing years ago, sat a mother and her children. Sure enough, they all turned to me with beet red, sweaty, pissed-off faces. People were honking at both of our cars now, screaming as they passed us, "Speed up!" Immediately, I felt protective over the slow-lane young mother and her brood, so I screamed back at each and every irate driver. *How dare they?* These were *my* people! Nobody in the air-conditioned crowd knew that this woman's hunk of burning junk was all she could afford, all they knew was that she was in their way. Unfortunately for the privileged crowd, I was going to make space for her. I kept close, honking loudly on her behalf until she rolled off at her exit. She smiled at me in the rearview, seemingly touched by my show of broken down, slow-lane solidarity. I understood this woman, when oddly enough, just the week before, I would have been too busy dream-driving all the passing Mercedes to even notice she was there. I felt like we were sisters, and in that moment, I wouldn't have traded my crappy car or the insight it had given me for a private jet.

I began to embrace life in the right lane, and I learned that driving slowly isn't the worst way to travel. When your ten-minute drive to work lengthens into a twenty-five-minute drive to work, you pick up on things that you might not have if you were zipping along in a luxurious Neon. As I rolled and bumped and stalled, I sang more songs, soaked up more of the sights, and best of all, could see I was not traveling alone. Plenty of people on that highway were like me: they drove less-than-perfect cars and led less-than-perfect lives. I came to love being a part of a motley crew of rusty-bellied trucks and low-riding sedans with duct-taped windows and no driver-side mirror. I looked out for vans precariously held together with bungee cords, because we were all on the same team, braving the daily grind and fighting the good fight. We waved to each other and smiled and forgave each other for the black cloudy flatulence our poor busted bumper cars spat into the air. I felt honored to be an official member of the Crappy Car Club. It wasn't easy, but nothing about life was.

When you join the Crappy Car Club, or the Hospital Waiting Room Club, or any club that has to do with cancer or disease, death or grief, betrayal or infidelity, financial ruin, addiction or depression—you join a club you had no idea existed. You join a club you probably never wanted to be a part of. You might hurt, you might be mad, you might even hope whatever the thing is that put you in the club gets taken from you and left in the desert, but no matter how bad club membership criteria becomes, you are never alone. Because you are not alone, you enter a wonderful world of empathy and sisterhood and solidarity. You grow deeper and get better. Even if you do end up with a Lexus one day, you'll always have compassion for the people driving the old slow cars. While the rest of the world honks and screams, you'll have the boldness to smile and wave. In fact, today you already have the power to make somebody else's drive or hurried lunch break a little bit easier.

Maybe those honkers and screamers didn't learn that famous quote in high school, "Be kind, for everyone you meet is fighting a hard battle." Maybe they're not in their "challenging" club just yet, but rest assured, they will be. Dramatic and tragic events happen to everyone, no matter what they drive or where they live, and when things get hard, we learn how much we need each other. Knowing the world is built on this system of give and take can be the greatest gift. Walking through the door to join this club you were meant to be part of to learn something from might be painful for a while, but we all journey down this twisting bumpy road of life together, at whatever pace. I'd like to welcome you, you belong here, to this Club of Life.

Chapter Five:
UNWANTED INTRUDERS

Life was hard, but good. At twenty-three years old, Mike and I were happily married, almost finished with school, and as a miraculous marker of adulthood, we were homeowners. Okay, technically we owned a condo in a sketchy complex, but the place grew on us. My dog and I took advantage of the two well-maintained swimming pools, which were usually empty; and, in the evenings, Mike and I enjoyed an especially good view of the always showy desert sunset. We had two bedrooms, two bathrooms, and a bunch of good friends who lived close by. There was an office space I could write in, and I proudly rolled around town scouring the ends of driveways on bulk trash day for the desk and chair that would perfectly fill it. A lot of our furniture was furniture other people were done with, and as we continued to make the condo space our own, we found ourselves on a first-name basis with employees at the local Goodwill.

Having a home filled us with confidence. It brought out the best in us. Two kids that used to depend on their parents were suddenly resourceful and tenacious adults. I found us a wobbly-legged kitchen table next to a dumpster, painted it black, and by the next week we were inviting friends for dinner and eating off of it. Mike

inherited a television and DVD player a few months in that facili-
tated countless movie nights and couch cuddles. To some people,
hearing us describe our condo as a "home" might have seemed a
bit of a stretch—we weren't exactly taking tea in the parlor—but
it was everything we needed. It was home and it was ours—until
they moved in.

Why does it seem that when we are in our happiest spaces,
when we've finally found our home, an intruder will come knocking on the door? Intruders are the pesky people, things, and feelings
that come into our most sacred spaces without invitation, permission, or welcome. Sickness, jealousy, an unexpectedly high elec-
tric bill—these intruders can make us feel invaded, attacked, and
insecure. Our feelings of safety and confidence fly out of orbit, and
before we know it, we're unsteady. An intruder who smashes your
car window and takes your phone is an awful nuisance, but it is
when we allow someone or something to take away our happiness,
that they truly become dangerous.

The intruders that came barging through our door had three
pairs of legs, floppy antennae, and thousands of friends.

A few months after Mike and I settled in the condo, the ten-
ants of the rental below us moved out. The U-Haul showed up, the
maintenance people, the painters, and then, pest control. I didn't
think much of it, because having an apartment fumigated seemed
like a routine precautionary task, especially for a landlord getting
ready to throw an empty unit on the market. I probably should
have asked the men entering the vacant apartment in hazmat suits
with their Ghostbusters packs on, "Hey, what's up?" I should have
called the landlord when the pest control team left the entire building smelling like citronella and hairspray, but I didn't. I probably
had yoga, or spinning, or pilates that day; I probably felt so safe
and secure in living my very best life that I couldn't even imagine

anything unseemly reaching us on our perfect, happy newlywed cloud. Within about a week though, my very best life went from bath bombs to bug bombs.

The first time we saw them, we had come home from a night out and flipped on the kitchen light. Mike and I were like Mom and Dad busting up a high school make-out party. They scattered. They bumped into the walls and disappeared into spaces we didn't know existed, under cabinets and into little cracks the walls. I specifically remember watching in horror as a gang of insects fled across the panini maker—*my panini maker!* The same panini maker that I had used every day for the past week to make my lunch. Panic set in, I dry heaved thinking about the germs I had most certainly ingested. I'd been cooking my food on a heated cockroach futon. A shell-like thorax brushed against my foot and as I leapt into Mike's arms, he leapt onto a chair. Even our little dog leapt—poor Oliver was horrified to discover the true identity of the heartless kibble bandits. It was official, the kitchen I was learning to cook in, the puffy cloud of home where we'd been feeling perfect, adult, and invincible, was under siege.

At first, we sprayed. We went to the hardware store on Saturday and picked the most potent insecticide we could find. The canister was fire engine red and pictured two belly-up roaches on the front. My husband and I high-fived, checked out, drove back to the condo, and showed no mercy! We felt proud, like a pair of fully certified, card carrying, extermination professionals. We promptly congratulated ourselves for "really handling the problem" by buying grocery store sushi and a used lamp for the living room. It was a good thing we were prompt in congratulating ourselves, because the triumph only lasted about forty-eight hours.

Two days later, while Mike was at work, I opened up the cupboard at lunch to find a multi-course roach feast, catered unknowingly by me, already underway. The little beasts were bolder this time too! They looked up at me from the Nature Valley Bars and Cheez-its and waddled slowly back into the darkness. I was shaking mad and ready to go nuclear, but I was also grossed out, defeated, and not at all ready to face them alone. I grabbed the dog and ran. Oliver and I waited outside the front door for two hours until Mike came home to save us or, at least, to try.

The cockroaches laughed in our faces, eating our mini-muffins and multiplying. We sprayed again, tried gels and baits and foggers, but it only made them breed harder. Before long, they were not only a disgusting problem, they were an expensive one too. We went into crisis mode. Mike and I held a very serious meeting/date night at our local Chipotle and began to discuss strategy. Meeting at home, we concluded, would only give the roaches an edge over us. Sitting over our burrito bowls and doing the math, we decided to hire a professional. Our bug spray budget was getting wildly out of control and at least a real bug guy wouldn't scream every time he opened the cupboards. We Yelp-vetted all of the local pest control companies and discovered that a man we'd always adored from our church was one of the best in town. It was a miracle. We called him, explained the situation, and he took pity us. He couldn't let two bright-eyed kids like us become hardened by life in a pest-riddled prison. He agreed to come see us first thing in the morning.

Exterminator Arvey showed up at our condo wearing a jolly old smile that very quickly faded. He whistled a long low whistle, and began worriedly poking around the plumbing and looking in the vents. We had no idea what was happening. At church, Arvey was usually chatty and friendly, but in our home, he had turned downright grim. When Arvey somberly asked if he could put a hole in one of our walls for a deeper roach probe, we knew we must be in very big trouble. When Arvey said he was going to need a few hours more to assess "the level of penetration," Mike and I packed our bags and went to stay the night with my parents. Roaches were literally forcing us out of our home.

When I arrived back at Mom and Dad's with my tail between my legs, I flopped onto the guest bed and let out a deep breath. Sometimes the powerlessness we feel in a lousy situation is even worse than the situation itself. The roaches were horrible, absolutely. The thought of this army of tiny intruders running around on me with their dirty little feet made me gag, but the feeling of being at their mercy was much worse. Mike lay down beside me and squeezed my hand, "What do you think they're doing in there right now?" he asked. "Watching Netflix and eating Doritos?"

I busted out laughing. In that ridiculous moment, I realized that thankfully, no matter what happened, there were some parts of our home that the intruders could never take away from us.

Mike and I being together made everything easier, but nothing was easy. Arvey called in the evening with bad news. We didn't just have a roach problem, we had an infestation. There were literally thousands of them in our walls, and they were spawning thousands of eggs. He said there were so many that he would have to come back in stages to kill them all. He would have to continue to administer treatments until there were no more mamas left to lay eggs. We were told it was going to get worse before it got better, and all we could do was be patient and get through it.

We moved back in, holding strong and standing together as the roach colony slowly took over every room of our house.

It was a contest of endurance—us versus them—and we knew that we just had to hold on a little bit longer. We counted down the days between pest treatments, ate our meals on the curb, and hung in there the best we could. No space was sacred, except mercifully, they never seemed to like the bedroom. One day, I picked up Oliver's food dish, and three roaches ran up my arm. The next day, I flipped on the bathroom light to find a proud mama roach with her babies on her back sitting on the shower drain and blinking at me. Mike heard me shriek, and he burst through the door while I sat curled up on the counter in a ball next to the toothpaste. We were so tired of the weird rotten lemon smell the chemicals left in our house. We were tired of sprinting to the safety of the bedroom the second we opened the door at night. We were tired of being forced off of our idyllic newlywed cloud. We were tired, but we had to keep going.

We live in a new cockroach-free home now, but in some ways, I'm glad we experienced those intruders. They somehow reminded me of all the things I had of incredible value: a loving set of arms to leap into when my heart was in my throat, and a humble home that is all mine to lacquer with as much insecticide as I wanted. I had friends and family who always made space for me, and I had the crazy good luck of having a Chipotle right down the street. Even if our newlywed cloud was half DEET, life was pretty fantastic.

Mike and I have continued to deal with unwanted intruders. Intruders have threatened our marriage and left me keeled over with anxiety; they divided our family and took complete control of our lives. We will continue to deal with various forms of intruders, and so will you. Though an intruder might never be welcome, they can bring welcome perspective. Pain, anxiety, and distress often leave us changed, but not all changes are bad. The roach rodeo revealed my ability to endure. Often, intruders will go away if you can outlast them. I've learned too that if you hang on long enough, even if an intruder takes up physical space, they can take up emotional space for only so long. They bet on the fact that you'll succumb to fear and insecurity, but they are the ones that scatter like bugs when you open up the door and face them. Try sitting in your fear, acknowledging it, honoring it, and waiting it out. Just ask that mama roach that I showered with. Resolve not to retreat and not to surrender, at least not until you've given yourself a chance to look your intruder in the eyes and say, "This space belongs to me.

Bugs are drawn to the energy, warmth, and shine of light. The fact that the roaches showed up was proof that Mike and I had something special, a home, a place of our own, a life we were working tirelessly and (mostly) joyfully to build. Intruders—bullies, relapses, diseases, fears—want nothing more than to bust down the walls of your home, your heart, and your health, because they know you hold something precious inside. When an intruder comes calling, remember the things you have that cannot be taken away. You have the power to endure, and you know that bugs are attracted to the light that belongs to you.

Walking into our house and seeing roaches for the first time scared me out of my heels. But not for one second did I regret turning on the light. That light helped me to see everything so much clearer, which meant I could do what needed to be done—I could take action.

Part Two:

YOUR LIGHT IS
CONTAGIOUS

Chapter Six:

THE BIG YES

Intruders do come barreling into our lives, but we mustn't forget that angels show up too. Sometimes, angels even show up in pairs.

Life presents us with beautiful gifts, wild opportunities, and incredible challenges. Often, we feel unprepared to acknowledge or accept them, so we don't. We say no to the new job on the other side of the country, no to a new love, no to a new learning environment, and no to trying the scary thing we believe we couldn't possibly do because we've never done it before. What would happen though if we stopped saying no all the time and began with one powerful "Yes!" instead?

My biggest "yes" adventure came at age twenty-five. Mike and I had been married for three years and out of college for a whopping 21 months. I was building my new start up, a jewelry company called The Shine Project, where I employed first-generation college students to help them pay for school. Mike was working his first full-time job. We had finally saved enough money to move out of the crime-ridden, roach-infested condo and into an actual house with normal neighbors and shiny floors. We were still young. We stayed up too late, our go-to dinner was still Chipotle with extra chips and guac, and we spent all of our expendable income at Urban Outfitters. We thought we were really crushing it in the real world. Our lives were busy and exactly as they should have been, full of exhaustion, hope, and excitement. We didn't know it yet, but we weren't entirely prepared for the opportunity that was coming our way. Not by a long shot.

A year before it happened, my sister Brooke and her husband moved out of state to pursue higher education. She got a part-time job to help with the bills and through it, became connected to two magical, adorable children. She quickly found herself spending a lot of time with them, taking them to the library and to lunch. My sister told us all about these kids over the phone, and we Facetimed them once so that they could show off the art projects they had made with her. The boy seemed fun and goofy; the girl was sugar sweet, but painfully shy. I didn't think too much of the relationship because my sister's Mary Poppins game had always been notoriously strong. Everywhere she went, kids adored her, so I figured she was simply stepping up to support a pair of busy, over-extended parents, as she had done with other families in the past. I had no reason to believe this time was any different, but I'd soon learn it was. These kids didn't come from a stable home, and my sister felt they truly needed her. Since they didn't have plans on Easter weekend, she offered to bring them to Phoenix to celebrate with our entire family.

"They've never been on an Easter egg hunt before!" she gushed excitedly to me on the phone.

My sister is adorable, loving, and endlessly trying to make things special for the people she cares for. She hatched a big plan to bring the kids to the exact same pastel-colored celebration we grew up going to. She was so gleeful, I thought she was going to explode into a ball of glitter.

"You and Mike *have* to come with us."

She was positively bubbling over, so we agreed.

At this time in our marriage, kids were not on the radar. We had just stepped into our careers and had no desire or intention of starting a family. We were not trying to become pregnant and had no interest in adoption or foster care. We had just gotten a dog, and that wasn't going very well. We weren't kid people. Neither of us had spent much time around children, and we weren't looking for opportunities to bond with a bunch of cranky, chubby-cheeked, sticky-palmed human beings. Regardless of the fact that we were feeling less than excited about being swarmed by little ones, we went to the Easter egg hunt because we'd promised we would. That morning, in the 95-degree, chocolate egg melting heat, something happened to me. Something changed. Everything changed in a split second.

S and Z bounded out of the car and stopped dead in their tracks. They looked around, taking it all in with their wide, chestnut-colored eyes: the big blue sky, the church building, and the strange adults they'd never met before smiling at them. They took tiny steps together, hand-in-hand, S leading Z around carefully like he'd just finished reading his big brother manual. He spoke for her when she couldn't get the words out herself. At age five, he was her guardian, her protector. They were the most perfect, clumsy, incredible, silly people I had ever seen. I knew right away with my whole being that we were connected somehow. When Z finally got the courage to tilt her chin upwards and look me in the eye, it was like being pulled in by an undertow. I was being tugged toward her by something invisible and divine. I knew immediately that I was going to be a part of their lives. These kids were profoundly familiar to me from the moment their shoes hit the dirt in front of me.

Not much blooms in the desert but when it does, it's the most achingly beautiful thing to behold. S and Z bloomed a little bit that day, and by lunchtime, investigative protective S was throwing his head back in laughter. He was letting us hold his sister's hand and lift her into our arms when her feet started hurting. Z, who in the morning, tiptoed around the lawn in complete silence, was talking a mile a minute about the Easter Bunny and showing me all of the treasures inside her pink plastic bucket. I felt so exhilarated and alive with them.

As we were getting in the car to leave, Z came running up the hill, her precious three-year-old face glowing and her brown springy curls bouncing. She yelled, "Wait for me, mama!!!"

I've replayed that scene in my mind a hundred times over the past five years. I will never un-hear those words.

Over the next twelve months, we continued to see S and Z. Whenever we road tripped to my sister's place, we would make sure to stop and see them too. We took them to the park and pushed them on the swings until their giggles became howls; we built pillow forts with them and read them stories about what happens when you give a mouse a cookie. We wiped their icky popsicle-stained fingers and dabbed their scraped knees with wet Bounty towels. We didn't really know what their life looked like at home, but we knew that we loved them and they loved us back. We knew we were *supposed* to love them. When my phone rang out of the blue one day, the voice on the other end of the line told me they wanted a better life for the children. The voice asked if Mike and I would raise S and Z.

I was completely unprepared for that moment and utterly uncertain of what to do in it. But, I said, "Yes!" with all of me. I wasn't a person to casually throw a gigantic word like that around. I immediately called Mike at work and asked, "Are you ready to be a dad to S and Z?"

I explained it all.

Mike answered with a strong yet shaky voice, "Yes. I've never been a dad, but I'll figure it out. I'll be the best dad to those kids that they could ever have."

We had every reason to say no, to say we weren't ready, to say that we needed time to get used to the idea of instant parenthood; but sometimes life says, "This gift is here for you." We decided to accept the gift, treasure it, and hold it in our arms, and say, "Yes Thank you."

Overnight, our family doubled. We welcomed the kids into our home and became their permanent legal guardians. We had no idea what we were doing, but we were doing it together, adventuring as a family of four. I frantically called my friends who had kids and rattled off questions.

"How often do I feed them? What snacks do I buy? They need car seats, right?"

It was confusing, exhausting, and thrilling. At the end of our second day together, we all piled into bed to read a nighttime story. It was only 7 PM, but as Mike read the first few pages of a brand new, never-cracked Dr. Seuss book, I fell asleep. I had never slept so peacefully. Life felt so full, so complete, so right, and so very unexpected. If I'd had more energy left, I would've shouted "Yes!" from the rooftops.

Because we said yes to the unknown, we were the recipients of a joy we never could have imagined. We got to experience little hands reaching for ours, first teeth lost, first days of school, and ballet recitals and soccer games. We found smashed Goldfish crackers in every corner of the house and car. We taught S and Z how to ride their bikes without training wheels while we were still learning to live without training wheels of our own. Unconditional almost unbearable love came to Mike and I because of a single word people don't use nearly often enough—*yes*. I don't know what made me brave that day on the phone or why taking more time to think it over felt so impossible, but I'm thankful that I didn't wait. The amount of growth, opportunity, joy, life, and love born in that one moment from that one word was enormous and profound. I want to go back in time hug my crazy younger self for doing the scary thing. I want tell her how proud I am of her for making a decision that she wasn't "ready" to make.

People thought we were nuts, but all the way along, God gave us the affirmations we needed. I remember the first time S called me Mom in public. They had been living with us for just six weeks and we were at the grocery store. The man scanning our items kept staring at me, then at the kids, then back at me. He finally asked the question we would hear countless times during our years together, "Is this your mom?" he asked the kids.

It was a question that held so much wonder, and so much nosiness. I didn't know how the kids would react, and I braced myself for them to be upset by it. Our life together was all so new and we were really just beginning to find our footing. S looked at me that day though with his big brown eyes. Smiling, he turned back to the man and said, "Yes, she is my mother."

He knew it and felt it. I knew it and felt it too.

I had felt like S and Z's mother a few weeks before when I pulled out the Legos and Barbies Mike and I had hastily bought for their toy chest before they arrived. I asked them if they'd like to play, and they looked confused. I started snapping the blocks together and, within a few seconds, S joined in. Deciding we would build a Lego castle for the Barbies, as the turrets got higher and higher, so did Z's squeals. S glanced at her and said, "Z, isn't this fun? We've never done this before!"

I wasn't sure what he was referring to, so I asked, "You haven't done *what* before?"

His response pierced me.

"We've never played like this together. It's just so fun."

I knew and felt it. These kids were home, and so was I.

In those early days, the kids followed me around everywhere, making sure I wasn't leaving, and curious as to whether or not they could fully trust they belonged with us. I became the person they called out for when they were sick or had a bad dream, the person they jumped up and down with when they did really well on a test or made a new friend, the person they wrote poems for on Mother's Day. Being Mom to them was life's greatest honor.

I want to be clear that I am not telling you to say yes to everything. That's not healthy, wise, or even possible; but, if your soul starts speaking to you, listen to her. If your heart begins to tug you in a direction you never expected, if it doesn't stop pulling you when you try and shake it, follow it if only for a few first steps. Don't say no to what could come next in your story before you have even looked at that blank page and imagined all of the beauty it could hold. Sit in the possibilities for a second; sit with the scary notions and the sad ones, but also with the ones that make your spirit soar. Ask yourself what would happen if you said yes to the next opportunity or challenge tossed your way? What would your life look like? More importantly, what would your life *feel* like?

Saying yes was scary for us. It didn't eliminate our fears; it magnified them. Being a parent is terrifying and heartbreaking! You see your children falter, hurt, and throw tantrums; you see them struggle between saying yes and no the way we all do. You stay up at night thinking about how dangerous the world is knowing that your heart is walking around outside of your body, just like your parent friends told you it would. But being parents also made Mike and I feel more awake and alive than we ever knew we could be.

Saying yes means you are willing to expand your path, take on new situations, and be challenged and tested. Saying yes is making a promise to yourself that you will dig deep for hope and comfort when the path gets mucky. Yes is an agreement to forge onward toward joy, growth, adventure, and the unknown. Yes is scary, but no is scarier. Saying yes doesn't eliminate fear, but it sure can help extinguish regret. Whether it's a first date, chopping off all your hair to a pixie style, learning to speak Italian, or becoming a parent overnight, the next time your life story presents you with a blank page, imagine all the newness it could contain.

Chapter Seven:
PLAYING PRETEND

"I'm 115 pounds! Same weight as I was freshman year. I did it!"

She was a senior varsity cheerleader. She had big, bouncy hair and big, bouncy boobs, and she was everything I wanted to be—the perfect embodiment of peppy blonde high school success. I was trying out for the team, wearing the wrong clothes, saying the wrong things to the other girls, and feeling like a complete fool. For some reason, they weighed us in front of each other, which was mortifying. I did not weigh 115 pounds, and everybody snickered as I stepped off of the scale. I had always been a tomboy. I didn't own a single pair of high heels or a bottle of Calvin Klein body spray, but I was a freshman now. I was ready to ditch my middle school bowl cut and grass stained baseball pants for a new uniform, the one that *she,* that perfect bouncy cheerleader was wearing.

The rules of high school had been hammered into my brain by every coming-of-age movie I'd ever seen, and I intended to follow them. You were supposed buy the new white platform Candies shoes Mandy Moore wore in *Seventeen* magazine; you were supposed to act like a woman even if you still felt like a girl; and you were supposed to be thin, pretty, popular, and desired. You were supposed to be a cheerleader.

At tryouts though, I could hardly jump off of the ground. The girls around me might as well have been on a trampoline. They flew up high into the air and corkscrewed their bodies, hugging their arms into their chests, and smiling maniacally from ear-to-ear. It was mesmerizing and humiliating all at once. I had never been to a dance class or taken gymnastics, and my lack of grace showed in every wobbly step I took. I felt like I was going to vomit. My knees were shaking, and the only way I would hold any value, any worthiness here, was if the judges and other girls accepted me onto the squad. Somehow, I had to make it work. Up again for my turn on the mat, I had sixty seconds to show everybody what I could do. As soon as Britney Spears started singing through the speakers one of the girls had brought, I took a shaky breath, leapt as high as I could, made a very uncheerleader-like grunt, and tried to touch my toes in the air. My legs slipped out from under me, and I landed flat on my back in front of laughing coaches and peers who knew what I kept pretending I didn't know: I wasn't supposed to be a cheerleader.

I got home that night with a purple bruise already forming on my behind. My ego in shambles, I quietly sobbed my way through a pot roast dinner. My sister Brooke sat across from me. She had long shiny doll hair, and she'd been on her middle school dance team since the moment she stepped through the gymnasium doors. Everyone loved her, and that day it was clearer than ever that she was destined to claim the identity I had fought so foolishly to make my own just hours prior.

"What's wrong, Ash?" she asked, twisting her beautiful mouth into a frown.

I told her exactly what had happened, from the weigh-in to the hopping across the gym like an exhausted toad, to the pièce de résistance, the toe touch.

"I'm never going to be a cheerleader," I pouted.

She started giggling her perfect musical-scale giggle and I wanted to smack her. But then, she said, "Good! That means you can be somebody that you actually want to be. You can be *you*."

Out of the mouths of little sisters!

Often, we make assumptions about ourselves, deciding who we want to be before we get the chance to discover who we are. We're wrong when we assume that we *have to* make the cheer squad, or get the job, or have the house full of kids to be happy and fulfill our destinies. We're wrong when we put the girl we think we should be up on a pedestal and put the beautiful girl that we are down. I imagined myself as a cheerleader, dreaming and committing to it. I envisioned myself prancing across that football field on Friday night blowing kisses to my beefy-shouldered boyfriend, and I refused to let go of that image. Because I was so fixated on becoming someone else though, I never got a chance to celebrate who I was: a good friend, an awesome outfielder, editor of the yearbook, a pretty incredible person who didn't even like dancing that much.

"Thanks," I spat at my sister, rolling my eyes. I didn't get the wisdom of what she'd said yet. I wouldn't get it until much later on.

At twenty-five years old with my toe-touching dreams behind me, I found a new narrative to commit to. I was supposed to be a businesswoman, an entrepreneur, a wearer of power suits, and an organizer of important meetings. I was set to take over the world, observing and mimicking female CEOs in *Time* magazine and downtown, standing in the shadows of big skyscrapers, tapping away on their BlackBerrys. These women were impressive, intimidating, and respected; they were everything I wanted to be. I worked until midnight, pounded the pavement looking for the right employees, tapped on my own BlackBerry, and wove my soul into The Shine Project. My business was my everything, my baby, my identity. I thought if I could be one of those women with an empire, a glass-walled corner office, and a staff that looked up to her, I would feel whole, happy, and validated. I thought if I could send thousands of young people to college, employ them, and give them resources they needed to be successful, I could earn a spot here on Earth. My life would be meaningful if I did all these things, but ultimately, the last thing I expected to bring me wholeness and fulfillment, came for me.

When S and Z came to live with us, I was deep in working woman mode. I was busy making my way out of the chrysalis, getting ready to spread my Ann Taylor Loft-clad butterfly wings and take the business world by storm. I was *not* looking to emerge from years of incubation and step straight into motherhood. That was never the plan. Suddenly though, motherhood was the reality. I was scared to be a mom and unsure how I would balance it all. What would I teach S and Z, and how? How would I care for them? Parenthood is not entirely instinctual.

I didn't know what these kids liked on their pizza or how many times a week it was okay for them to eat it. I worried that this enormous motherhood business was going to get in the way of my entrepreneur metamorphosis and keep me from becoming the woman I was supposed to be. Oh, how wrong I was! Motherhood made my metamorphosis possible. Motherhood, the unexpected plot twist in my carefully composed narrative, allowed me to shine my brightest.

In those early days of family, S and Z thought they knew who they were supposed to be too. They were tough, they did their best to show us they didn't need us, and they were very slow to trust. I didn't know how we would reach them. I didn't view myself as a patient, nurturing, or very good teacher, but somehow, I found my way. The parts of myself I thought were weakest, ended up being my greatest strengths.

One afternoon, Z was struggling to buckle herself into the strange, stiff, brand new car seat we had bought her. We were going to the store that day, and I had promised the kids they could pick out any ice cream they wanted. Propelled by the promise of mint chocolate chip, Z hurled her little body into the car and got to work securing her harness. She fumbled around, huffing and puffing while her brother urged her on.

"Go faster, Z! Ice cream! Come on!"

Her hands were shaking. She was so excited, but she couldn't figure how the clasps worked. In seconds, her laughter collapsed into expletives, and I heard her angry four-year-old voice rattle off a four-letter word.

You could have heard a pin drop in the backseat. Z knew she was in trouble and S did too. Both kids' eyes widened as they braced themselves, waiting for the punishment to fly off of my tongue the way it always did when they acted out of line. I didn't know what to do. Was I was supposed put Z in a time out, ignore her, or laugh (her expression really had been so funny and earnest)? Finally, a calm settled over me, and I knew exactly what to do.

"Z," I began. "Do you know why we don't say those words?"

She shook her head no, so I went on to explain, in gentle toddler terms, how language can hurt people. I gave her some different choices to use, and she tried them all out.

"Dang! I'm mad! Chicken!" (The last option was just for fun.)

Z wasn't in trouble, she wasn't criticized, and she wasn't yelled at. She was taught. I unbuckled my own seatbelt and reached back to buckle hers, giving her pudgy little hand a squeeze on the way.

My six-year-old son was in complete shock. The sequence of events that had transpired as we idled in the driveway stood in contrast to everything he thought he knew about adults.

"Wow, you have the voice of an angel," he said. "You didn't even yell or get us in trouble."

As I began to feel the kids' confidence in me growing, I felt my own confidence growing too. In little moments—such as the car-seat-swear-word moment—we established the very beginnings of trust, safety, and respect. I showed S and Z that it was okay to make mistakes, to learn, and grow. No decision they could make would ever cause me to love them more or less. My love for them was constant and unconditional.

The kids revealed parts of me that stood in opposition to everything I thought I was. I could teach, lead, and provide the type of support and encouragement they needed to feel safe and at peace. I'm not sure I've ever been more excited about a venture, prouder of a role, or more affirmed in a purpose, as I was that day in the car. I had spent my whole life looking outward—searching for the kind of person I ought to be and for the person that would elevate me to greatness—but what if the greatness we are all searching for has never really been "out there?" What if the greatness is already inside of us?

In motherhood, I flourished. We all did. It took time—S pushed the boundaries for months, yelling, fighting, and misbehaving. He was trying to see if we'd still be there to love and care for him, no matter what he did. The more he pushed us away though, as exhausting as it was, the wider we opened our arms to him. Whenever either child made a bad choice, we reminded them of the good choices they had made. Whenever they talked down to themselves or each other, we built them back up. Every glorious flash of kindness I saw—S pouring Z a glass of water, Z taking the fall for S when he was clearly the one who etched the stick figure with the crown into the new dining room table—felt like an accolade. Every new thing we helped them discover about themselves was a discovery, a victory, for all of us.

S was a great storyteller, he loved reading, and he was scared of being let down. Z was a thinker, she loved God, church, and all the animals, and you couldn't cuddle her enough. I was the mother of two incredible, inspiring children. This role of a lifetime was the one I had always been waiting for. Motherhood made me a better daughter, a better wife, and even a better businesswoman. I learned to communicate and lead, I learned to teach, and I witnessed daily the importance of positive reinforcement. I learned how to balance my time and my expectations.

When people learned we had taken in two children who weren't ours biologically, some would say, "Wow, you just really changed their lives. They are so lucky to have you." It irked me, because the kids weren't the "lucky" ones, Mike and I were. I learned to love more fully. In being stretched to capacity and pushed to the brink, I was rewarded beyond measure in the joyful work I was privileged enough to take on. What S and Z gave to me and taught me, I couldn't have learned anywhere else. I will carry them with me always. I will wonder, always, why more women don't put "Mother" at the very top of their resume.

Sisters, there is greatness in you. Look inward at who you are, instead of outward at someone you aren't. There are a lot of options on display here in the world, and it is easy see the cast of characters and commit to the role you think you want, but what if your "plan" keeps you from discovering the role you were always meant to play? If you spend your life playing pretend, your happiness will be pretend too.

Don't let that happen. Get to know the wonderful woman you already are, place *her* on the pedestal, give her a chance, and respect and nurture her. In motherhood, I found joy, challenge, and complexity. I developed a deeper understanding of love and life. I became a successful businesswoman, and you know what? I became pretty decent cheerleader too.

Chapter Eight:
GUARDIANS

My son and I were hiking one day. It was his half-day at school, and we both looked forward to this outdoor time every week. After I picked him up, we would drive across town to our favorite special spot and go on an adventure, just the two of us. The best trail is right behind my parents' house. It starts in a desert wash, a dry streambed with divots and corduroy grooves carved by water that would rush whenever, if ever, it rained.

Nature was different down there in the wash. S and I would spot the things normally hidden from us—baby coyotes, roadrunners, and bright green lizards. We'd see vegetation that didn't exist in the city. Before we began our big trek up South Mountain, we would stand down there in the cradle for a while and take it all in before forging on and heading up and over.

As S got older, it took us less and less time to reach the peak. I always wished I could make the journey last longer than it did. In some way or another, I think all mothers feel that way when their children start to grow up and everything, including the children themselves, starts to move too fast. S was a talker, and if he got on the right topic, it would slow down his pace a bit. Each time we hiked, I'd time how long he would jabber away before I finally got a word in so Mike and I could smile about it later, after S and Z were in bed. Once, he spoke a full hour and fifteen minutes. An avid listener, I loved the chattiness, I was his biggest fan. Whether the topic of the day was the new unsanctioned Harry Potter spinoff he was writing, or how he sold origami at school and made $15, I just couldn't hear enough. He was so brilliant, so eager to soak up life and learning, and all he needed was for me to be there to simply listen.

Of course, he also needed extra reassurance at times, which is true of a lot of children who end up in a different home with a different family than the one they started out with. I always told him that I loved him and he belonged with us, and because this truth made him feel so good, he wanted to give that kind of validation back to us too. He was a fierce protector, a model older brother, and the kind of kid who valued loyalty in a friend over whether or not they had a swimming pool. The older he got and the more he saw of the world, the more he realized that our family—or, our "situation" as it was so often, too often, put to him—was different.

It was a Wednesday when we set foot into the wash for our routine march across the shriveled, empty marsh. He was upset by something that happened in his classroom and he wasn't his usual happy self. I didn't want to prod him, so I waited. After a few minutes, he spoke.

"Mom, today they gave me a paper that called you my 'legal guardian.'"

Technically, we were S and Z's legal guardians, but he only knew us as "Mom and Dad." The title "guardian" felt "less than" familial to him. It did to Mike and I too. Anytime we heard it or saw it on a piece of mail, we would shudder. It made us feel like babysitters when, in all aspects of our lives, we were parents. Now, those words made S shudder too. More than anything, our protective, loving boy valued the safety and security of his family. Those words, no matter how little weight they carried in our hearts, seemed threatening to him. We were the LeMieuxs. All of us were LeMieuxs. None of us liked being called anything different than "a family." S stomped his feet so hard while telling me about this paper that dust flew up into our faces.

I stopped him for a moment so I could crouch down and explain something to him I'd had to explain to myself many times before.

"S, all parents are guardians. It's our job to protect our children, and that's exactly what your dad and I do. We are just like every other mom and dad, like the ones all of your friends at school have."

S looked me straight in the eye and grimaced. For some reason, my explanation or the words "legal guardian" just didn't feel right to him. If I'm being totally honest, it didn't feel right to me either.

On the hike up South Mountain, there is a point that always made me nervous. It's a switchback, a little trail zig-zag which helps prevent erosion, and although it seems easy enough, when you're more than 1000 feet up, one small slip or stumble in the wrong direction could be fatal. I told S to watch his step and did what I always did when the path started to narrow and change direction—I became his shadow. I walked right behind him so, if necessary, I could reach out and grab him. All the primal mothering instincts intensified as I tried to master the tricky balance between letting my kid feel strong and independent, and wanting to scoop him up and carry him through the rough parts like a baby.

S cruised forward past saguaro cacti and fat lizards, all the while continuing a passionate monologue about the new recess club he and his best friend had created. I nodded while he told me all of the rules they had drawn up to govern their adorable new organization. I was half-listening, half-watching him like a hawk when his right foot skidded. He caught his toe on a rock, and then he made a scared little "meep" sound and started to slip. Reflexively, I reached out and grabbed him. It wasn't any type of dramatic fall, just your average kid bail. Had I not been there, he probably would have scraped his knee and gotten back up again without missing a beat. But, as he faltered and I reacted, something clicked in his constantly churning, boy-genius brain. S peeked back at my hand still locked around his arm and smiled. He had the most confident and peaceful look on his face. He understood he was safe and my instinct was and always would be to protect him and reach out for him when he needed me—even if he didn't know that he did. My heart was spasming under my shirt, and my breath was ragged when he spoke the truest, sweetest words.

"Mom," he said. "I know why you're called my guardian. It's because you protect me. You protect me from getting hurt, from bad things, and you keep me safe. Of course you're called my guardian! 'Guardian,' I love that word."

Suddenly, it didn't seem like such an indignity anymore—being a guardian. It seemed absolutely perfect. In that moment, halfway up a big dusty hill in the middle of Phoenix, my nine-year-old son revealed the glory of who I was, who *we* were. Together we were a protector and her treasure, an artist and her greatest work, a mother and her son. He taught me that the word "guardian," the word that had haunted me and made me feel self-conscious, less mother and more warden, was actually the greatest title I could possibly be given. Somebody out there or up there trusted me to teach, celebrate, mother, and care for these beautiful, magical, important human beings. Of all the people in the world, that sacred post was passed on to me. S had a realization too. For the first time, I think he truly saw how supported he was. He realized there was someone who looked after him and would be there if he fell. He had seen so much change in his short life, but that day was monumental in that he realized he would be loved and protected forever. To him, I might as well have been Wonder Woman.

When we got down the mountain and picked Z up from school, the second she was buckled into her booster, S told her the big news. "Z! Do you know that Mom and Dad are our guardians?!" Z's eyes seemed to fill with stardust, the way they always did when her big brother shared a piece of important information with her.

"Coooooooool" she sang back at him. "Mom, you're a gaaaaarden!"

I couldn't get home fast enough to share the revelation with Mike, who upon hearing about the Near Peril on South Mountain, loudly cleared his throat, blew his nose, and worked very hard not to weep. We watched hand-in-hand as S, always a big researcher, took the hardcover dictionary off of the bookshelf and asked us how to spell that word they called us again. We helped him find it right between *guardfish* and *guardrail* and he read to us, slowly. His voice filled with awe.

"The word 'guardian' means a defender, protector, or keeper. Woooooow!"

Z giggled and "Woooooooowed" too.

"You guys are the coolest. My mom and dad are the coolest!

He was right: we were the coolest. We were his guardians. We were his sister's guardians. We were the defenders of their lives, we protected them from harm, and we were a wellspring of love, hope, and security they could drink from whenever they needed, until the end of time. This newfound knowledge about our identity thrilled S and Z, and it thrilled us too. It filled us up with confidence, purpose, and determination that made the early days, back when I was still struggling to understand my role, feel like a million miles away.

In the months that followed, S became obsessed with the concept of guardianship. No longer confused by it, he was proud of it.

Mike and I grew increasingly prouder of the concept too. It was so sweet to bear witness to S's interpretation of it at play in the world. He called himself the "guardian" of the bearded dragon, Zachary, that we had given him for his birthday. He cared for Zachary like the fate of the free world depended on the physical and emotional wellbeing of a lizard the size of a running shoe. He would clean his cage, feed him at all mealtimes, and tell us when he was running dangerously low on crickets. To the shock and horror of our neighbors, he even took the scaly beast for walks down the street using a lizard leash. At nighttime once, I overheard him wish Zachary a goodnight, and with all the sincerity and tenderness in the world, tell him that he would always be there to love and protect him. Just like kids, by the way, bearded dragons are completely dependent on their human for about eighteen years. And no, nobody at PetSmart told us this until after we had checked out.

S also began to call himself one of Z's guardians too. He took a special interest in teaching her things, whether it was about spaceships, Legos, or the best kind of string cheese. He would hold her hand if we were in the mall and tell her not to be nervous when the lights dimmed in the movie theater. If she heard a strange noise or felt vulnerable, she would curl her body into his on the couch, and he would assure her that everything would be okay. In truth, S had been her guardian long before we became a family; the only difference now was that he could do so with the absolute confidence everything *would* be okay. Brother and sister were safe, secure, and so loved.

As more letters from the school came home to us in backpacks, and notices from the state filled our mailbox, the word "guardian" stopped jumping off of the page at me. It didn't feel like an insult, a typo, or an oversight—it felt like the greatest privilege. To be honest though, I had already stopped worrying so much about what words people used to describe us at that point. Trust me, when you're a young white couple who suddenly has two brown children, you hear some memorable stuff. Mike and I had heard everything from "aunt and uncle" to "temporary parents" to "friends" to describe what we were to our children. It took some adjusting at first, but eventually all of it rolled off our backs. What others *called* us didn't mean anything; what we *were* to each other meant the world.

So often we try to define our identities and relationships with the right word or phrase. We want to be something easy to Google and understand. But, sweet friends, we aren't easy to understand at all. We are complex beings subject to complex dynamics laid out in a really, really complex world. A label might help us feel more secure or grounded. Categorizing ourselves might make us understand ourselves, our jobs, or our relationship with God better, but trying to live up to somebody else's definition of what we are limits who we can be.

If you do have a title attached to you the way a lot of us do, like "wife" or "boss" or "guardian," know that you get to be the one to define what your title means. It doesn't matter if "mother" or "woman" means something different to everybody else. That day on the mountain, as we walked and talked through hot, red dust clouds, S gave me the courage to redefine myself as a mother and as a woman. He gave me the perspective I needed to reimagine something I saw as a weakness as the most formidable strength. Readers, don't let anybody tell you what you are—show everyone who you are.

Part Three:

YOUR LIGHT WILL
GET HEAVY

Chapter Nine:

THE FIGHT

The closest, logical thing I could throw up in was our kitchen sink. My husband was holding me up with every ounce of strength he had. My legs were made of pudding. I had no control over them. I cried. I yowled like a dog. I grabbed frantically to whatever I could to keep the explosive grief from sending both Mike and I straight to the floor.

They wanted to take our children. They were trying to take our children from us.

Just two months prior, we felt it was time to finalize the adoption of S and Z. We answered to Mom and Dad, volunteered at the school, threw doll tea parties, built Lego masterpieces, and made all the nightmares, bullies, and booboos go away. We belonged to each other, and after three years of belonging to each other, it was time to make it official. The kids could not have been more on board. They had chosen to take our last name as their own, our parents were their grandparents, and our dog was their dog. Adoption was the next natural step, and we were all excited to take it together. We hired an attorney who convinced us the route we were taking to adopt the children was the right and only way. He said the process would be quick, mostly just paperwork.

Sitting across from him during our first meeting, I had a feeling, a "mom" feeling, a primal, instinctual fear that made the worst-case scenario appear on the horizon.

"There's no way we'd lose the children, right? There's nothing that could make that happen, is there?"

I didn't really know what I was referring to, if it were even possible for permanent legal guardians to lose custody, but I had to ask. Something in my bones was begging me to. The lawyer smiled and assured me nothing would split our family apart. It was all supposed to be easy. So, when the letter came, I was beside myself.

We had just put the kids to bed and were getting ready to spend October break in Canada. Family vacations were our favorite moments of the year, and we only had seven more sleeps until the kickoff of our fall adventure in Banff. I went on a short walk to the mailbox because we hadn't had time for our daily dog walk/mail grab routine after school. I remember thinking about how tall S was getting and wondering if I should put the humidifier on in Z's room. I dropped the stack of mail on the table when I got inside and started sorting through it. I was surprised to find a letter from the juvenile court system, from the same judge who granted us permanent guardianship years before. I wasn't concerned, because as a guardian of children, every year you have to give a status update. They then send you a short letter back that more or less reads, "Yes, you are still guardians. Thank you." I was sure that was what I was tearing into, but I was wrong.

"Your guardianship is terminated."

The words instantly started to blur. My head pounded. A court date. An official seal. It was a mistake; it had to be, right? Maybe our yearly paperwork had gotten lost in the mail, or the clerk had misfiled something and sent us the wrong letter. Maybe our status had been upgraded from "guardians" to "parents." But it was too soon for that. It took a minute, but when reality hit me, it hit like a bullet. Our adoption was being contested.

The biological family members who originally granted us our permanent guardianship were now filing to take it away. They wanted the kids back. Our kids.

I sat on the couch, completely frozen. It was quiet in the house except for the sound of the paper shaking in my hands as I read it again and again and again. None of it made sense. Everything started to slowly spin.

How can something 'permanent' become temporary so easily?

Why would anyone contest this?

What does this mean?

Am I about to lose my children?

I ran over to the kitchen sink and threw up, giving into the deep ache in my stomach and letting it hollow me out. Mike came running down the stairs. He wrapped his arms around me while I heaved and heaved with my head in the sink until there was nothing left. Afterwards, I handed him the letter.

There we stood, in our kitchen, disintegrating. Images and evidence of our family danced around us—lunchboxes, Crayola marker artwork tacked to the fridge, still those Goldfish crackers, and so many, many photographs. In an instant, we were confronted with what we could lose and with the reality of what we had just entered into: the biggest fight of our lives.

A knock on our door came one Wednesday afternoon, two months after the fight began. I had never seen this visitor before and had no advanced warning that she was coming. She stumbled over her words like she had no idea why or how she had ended up on our stoop either. I had to ask to see her credentials before inviting her in. She was a caseworker for the Department of Child

Safety. They were opening an investigation, and she had come to our home to interview the children.

This was to be the first of many times I would stand face-to-face with an opponent. The fight had landed on my doorstep, and now I was being forced to let it inside. I tried to stay strong for the children and for myself. This woman had done nothing to directly attack me, but she was the thumbnail of a bigger, scarier picture. The state was getting involved. No matter the history or the cost, the primary goal of DCS is to reunite children with their biological families—and of course, Mike and I and S and Z were not biologically connected. We were now stuck in a broken system governed by broken laws, a system none of us could ever had imagined we'd be a part of. We were not foster parents; we were parents. I was Mom, Mike was Dad, and with S and Z, we were a family. Anyone working against this was just so wrong.

The woman from DCS waltzed around our house looking at the art on the walls and the fruit in the fruit bowl while I stood by, furious. I was seething, actually. I could hear the sound of my teeth locking together and my jaw tightening.

"Department of Child Safety?" I wanted to scream, but I couldn't.

My children were watching me the way they always did, trying to figure out if they should be angry or afraid too. I absolutely did not want to place that enormous burden on their shoulders. They were sitting on the couch watching this stranger examine our home. When she finally leaned down to them to say hello, they looked at me for reassurance, and I nodded. They said hello back to her. With a grin on her face, the woman asked me to leave the room. She said she needed to meet with *the* children, my children, alone. As I began to walk away, toward detention in my own house, an image appeared that still haunts me. With each step I took away from S and Z, I saw their glowing faces dim and their eyes lose their light. The giggles, the joy, and the confidence they had built with us faded to terror, confusion, and mistrust. I heard them sobbing quietly as she asked them question after question. They were trying so hard to be brave.

After a full hour, the woman left. She gave me a mechanical handshake and said" goodbye" cheerily to the kids. Financial services packets and hotline numbers were shoved at me, and she awkwardly explained that it was routine for her to drop these off with every visit, whether I needed them or not. It dawned on me that no matter how different our case was, we were being lumped into the 18,000 other active child welfare cases in the state of Arizona. We were just another item on a stranger's to-do list. S and Z's wet swollen eyes darted from my face to hers, and she walked out the door. It was as though she couldn't even see their tears, like she was totally untouched by their sadness. When she left, they fell apart.

"She asked me what family I love more."

"She said I had to choose one. And I can't. But she made me, and I don't want to talk about it ever again."

S flopped into my arms and in that moment, it started to sink in. I could feel the hatred, the poison, and the vitriol rolling over me like hot wind. The social worker, whose job it was to protect my children, had made them feel unsafe. She had the nerve to place this weight on their little seven and nine-year-old shoulders, knowing they could not carry it. I would watch them struggle under that burden for months.

"Baby, I'm so sorry this is happening and that those questions were asked. I want you to know that you don't have to choose. Hearts are made big enough so you can love all of the people you want to love. There's no choice to be made. That's like asking me who I love the most out of the two of you. It's a question that has no answer because love cannot be measured, nor is it supposed to be. I'm just so sorry."

Z sidled up to us, and we all huddled together. I *was* sorry. I had never felt more enraged, more ready, or more willing to go to war for my children. As their tired little bodies leaned into mine, I was confronted with a question: What do you bring to the biggest fight of your life?

You can bring lots of things to a fight. You can bring anger, fear, and pain; you can bring aggression, hatred, or all-out rage. You have all of these very powerful tools at your disposal. But you can also bring something more potent and commanding than all of those elements combined: love.

That afternoon, as I held my children and helped them try and sort through emotions that were too big for them—too big for all of us—darkness set in. As I watched the woman who had brought this terror and gloom into our living room climb into her little red car and drive off to disrupt the next family, I felt fury, dread, panic, and pain. At the same time, I was overwhelmed and shocked at how love—the purest, most potent and immaculate love I had ever felt—was beginning to swallow all my worst thoughts. Moving forward, I would let the love of my children guide me. I would learn to use it in ways I never knew I could. My love for them ignited something in me, and I would not allow that light to dim—I would nourish it so it would flourish like fire.

During the proceedings, we weren't legally allowed to speak publicly about what was happening. We weren't allowed to breathe our children's names. Z and S—our best adventurers, our children—disappeared from my social media, from our Christmas card, and from our mouths. The loneliness of our battle was overwhelming, but in the loneliness, a cocooning kind of strength was born. I have never loved harder, shone brighter, or given more of myself to something. The first day in court, I put on my most grown-up work clothes and faced the people who were trying to rip our family to shreds. When I looked in their eyes and they looked in mine, I felt anger. I listened as lawyers in shark suits told horrific manufactured lies and felt disgust. I took depositions in front of strangers and felt fear. Yes, all of those negative feelings were present and enormous, but they were insignificant compared to the love I had for what I was fighting for: the sacrosanct bond of family.

The court battle nearly leveled us. It was one of the most destructive times in our lives, and we were skinny, exhausted, and sick with worry. The stomach pain, the deep empty pit that showed up that day in the kitchen, never went away. I could hardly eat a full meal or sleep through the night without running to the bathroom. This gnawing pain enveloped me on hearing days, whenever our attorney called, and whenever someone from the state showed up unannounced at our door. The millstone was so heavy my body could hardly support it. Everything about my physical self and spirit felt on the verge of collapse. I didn't break though. Because we fought with wild, infinite, love, a system designed to make us weak only made us stronger. Mike and I had become part super-hero, through no choice of our own.

I could write an entire separate book on the pain and injustice the four of us experienced in those seventeen months in court, but I choose a different story: Love. Bring love to the biggest fights of your life. If you fight with love, you are unstoppable and unbreakable. If you fight with love, you fight with fire. If you fight with love, you have the courage to keep showing up. Love kept me going. Love pushed me to keep showing up to a dank, lonely, and anxiety-ridden court room. Love allowed me to create an environment in the midst of the nightmare, where my kids could be kids, where my kids could be joyful and thriving. Love pulled me up after being knocked out over and over again. Love transformed the tiniest spark in me to full-force explosiveness. I had always known I could shine, but I never knew I could shine quite like I did for S and Z.

If you are reading this and struggling, if you're facing your deepest hardship and feeling like you're not enough, I'm so sorry. Nobody goes looking for a fight, and I know you've come to yours with a heavy heart. I know the pain of unanswered prayers hitting the ceiling, of wondering if you'll ever feel joy again, of asking yourself if the fight is even worth it. I want you to know I see you, I feel for you, and I stand with you.

You are part of a very big club now, remember? You may feel fear, anger, and pain; you may be exhausted; and you may be throwing up in your kitchen sink; but I implore you to go deeper to root of your pain. Once you dig past the ugliness and muck, you will find love. If you do love something so much that you're willing to go to war for it, and you are willing to sacrifice your sanity and allow your heart to be broken—how amazing is that? How beautiful and mind-boggling? Anger and hurt will burn you out, but love will sustain you. Let love be the force that fuels your fire and see how long it smolders. I believe you will be just as wonderstruck and grateful as I was.

Though I wish I could, I cannot promise you your love will win you all of your battles. No matter how hard you try, how long you stay standing, and how many times you pull yourself up from the muck, you'll still lose from time to time. You can't control who wins every fight, but you can control who shows up for it. Besides, it isn't your job to win, though I know when your home, or job, or kids are on the line, it can feel as though it all comes down to you. But no, it's bigger than that: God calls the fight. That's His job. Your only job, sweet sister, is to keep showing up and feeding that glorious fire of yours. By showing up, you claim victory over one thing: regret.

The next time you find yourself in the middle of a fight falling face down toward the mat, the next time you feel anger, hatred, or grief, remember you wouldn't be fighting at all if there wasn't something worth fighting for. Love is the only thing you need to bring to a fight, and love is the thing most worth fighting for.

Chapter Ten:
DON'T FORGET YOUR COURAGE

I told Z that I was on my way to the office that morning, but she knew I was lying. We were in the middle of our court battle, and the weight of it was starting to crack me wide open. She looked up from her oatmeal, let out a little sigh, and stared deep into my eyes. She could sense something was different that day. Z could always tell when something was going on with me; we were connected that way. This little girl was my best friend and my shadow. Whenever I was scared, frustrated, or preoccupied, no matter how hard I tried to bury it under the surface, she was always able to see me. She would fix those wise, steady, baby owl eyes on me until I fessed up or melted completely in her light. She was my soulmate, and our twin spirits shone so bright together that people on the street would tell us we looked exactly alike—even though we had totally different skin colors. From the moment I saw her, I felt like I had always known her, my life before her didn't exist, and neither would a life exist if she disappeared. Ours was an eternal love, immune to the constraints of time and space. It still is. To experience and know Z was to enter into a new world of hope, life, and purpose. To love her was to learn to live courageously.

As I headed to the door that morning, after kissing the kids goodbye, Z said, "Mama! Don't forget your courage."

I took a deep breath, smiled, held my head a little higher, and walked out the door with my husband. To this day, I remember where our girl was standing, the look on her face, the little spot on her shirt where she spilled her milk, and her radical, incredible bravery. She was trying to stand tall and strong for her mama, even though she did not understand why I needed her to do it.

Every Saturday, we cuddled up as a family on the couch with a giant bowl of popcorn (and at least thirty stuffed animals surrounding us) to watch something special. A movie called *We Bought A Zoo* was our favorite, we must have watched it two dozen times. The four of us would usually sit within arm's reach of each other, no matter how squished and sweaty we got. I'm not sure any of us ever said the words aloud, but Saturday couch time was our most cherished time of the week. The family in *We Bought a Zoo* had recently lost their mother—their beacon—and the son was grieving. At one point, the father, played by Matt Damon, explains to his son the power of wild unrestrained courage.

I was sitting next to Z when we heard that explanation for the first time. This view of courage made sense to us. Eating chips while Matt Damon preached to us from the flat screen, we sat there nodding in tandem. In our toughest moments, all we had to do was be brave, even if only for a flash.

Courage became a part of our special mother-daughter language. Courage was our daily mantra. Whenever she was faced with a challenge, I would say, "Z, don't forget your courage today! Baby girl, that is all you need to bring. When it gets hard, take a deep breath, and find it within yourself."

She would then close her eyes hard and open them, totally reignited.

When going to school caused her great anxiety, I reminder her, "Don't forget your courage!"

At the height of our custody battle, I would look in the bathroom mirror of the courthouse and remind myself, "Ashley, don't forget your courage."

When our door bell rang unexpectedly, and I knew I'd find another case worker with a clipboard full of forms on the other side, I would pause a minute before opening the door, just long enough to tell my kids, "Be strong, be honest, and don't forget your courage."

Waking up every morning only to be hit with our reality all over again, Mike and I clung to this.

"We can do this as long as we don't forget our courage."

It might seem silly—or fruitless—but consciously igniting our courage made us all stand a bit taller. Throughout the day, as we weathered our separate storms, I would picture my counterpart Z taking a deep breath at her desk, and it would give me the power to do the same. I was always taught that courage was big and loud, but Z was small and quiet and the bravest person I had ever met. Here is a sampling of what she taught me about wild, empowering, glorious, and unforgettable courage:

Courage hurts. Courageousness is not about earning an exemption from pain and fear. It's about accepting their invitation to meet. Courage is showing up to what scares you, invitation in nervous hand, and stepping over the threshold. Courage is not easily accomplished, and often, the process of attaining it is not very fun. What courage is though, is illuminating. The second you say yes to the invitation to walk through the door of any challenge, you strike a deal with yourself, acknowledging what lies beyond fear even when you're in the midst of it.

My first day of court was the most terrifying day of my life. I took a deep breath, held my head high, and walked through the rain on the only rainy day Phoenix had seen in months. I was holding onto Mike's hand for dear life. The huge heavy doors of Juvenile Court were the only thing standing between me and my deepest fear. I passed through those doors, I passed through the metal detector on the other side, and I accepted my invitation. I acknowledged not only the great fear, but also the great hope of that first day. It took courage to sit in that hall on the cold plastic chairs that made me itch. It took courage to run to the bathroom, throw up, and come back out again when I saw that we were up next. It took courage to lock eyes with a young boy in foster care who was anxiously waiting to appear before the judge, without any parents by his side, and silently send him a *"We can do this. We are brave."*

Everyone was brave there; we had all shown up. A hallway full of youth with no family to take care of them and with no choice to do anything but to be there—scared and alone—is the picture I will see for the rest of my life whenever I think of courage.

Courage requires breathing. Whatever adversity you face, being awake to your inhale and exhale is the quickest way to remind yourself, "Hey, I'm still here, I'm still going, I'm still full of life." When you're frozen on a stage about to speak to 6,000 people, or standing before a judge who holds the rest of your life in his hands, or walking down the aisle on your wedding day, the simple act breathing can feel like a quantum physics experiment.

Z often reminded me that her name means life. She would look at me square in the eyes, hold my face with her little hands and say, "I give you life, don't I, Mama?"

It was never really a question, but a confident statement. She did give me life. She was electrifying and joyful and inspiring from the second she opened her beautiful eyes in the morning to the moment she shut them and drifted off to sleep. Sometimes I would just hold her, rocking her back and forth and listening to her breathe. She kept me grounded, and nothing else in the entire world mattered when I held her there in my arms. She made me feel alive and connected to a greater calling and purpose. Breathing her in brought me true joy. Being in her midst made me brave.

When I was waiting to be deposed, I would sit there on the stand breathing, imagining Z in my lungs. I would meditate on her, reminding myself that I was alive, courageous, and ready. Breathing kept me focused on what mattered, and so sisters, I ask you to breathe for me right now. You are here, you are living, you are enduring. Anytime you forget those absolutely astonishing truths, you'll find them at the bottom of a deep breath. Sometimes, we fight so hard to merely survive we forget to do the simple things keeping us alive. Life and courage all start with breathing.

Courage always starts small. That's how you know courage is real and there to stay. You build it brick-by-brick, step-by-step. Sometimes, courage is illustrated as a big showy production, but that's just fear in a pretty dress. Real courage doesn't masquerade itself and pop out from behind a curtain—it evolves. It is real, honest, and true.

Z's courage started the second she slept in her own bed the first night in her new home. That small act was the beginning of great bravery and growth. She found courage on her first day of preschool, and she found it the day she trusted us enough to call us Mom and Dad. She continued to find it during the fight, when she chose to live fully and seek joy even through confusion. Over the course of just a few years, the little girl who once followed me around every corner of the house not wanting to be left alone became a dancer who shined on stage at competitions. I would watch, tears dripping down my cheeks, as my shy baby turned and smiled, performing for a crowd of hundreds. She was a leader in her dance group and in every place beyond, all because she let her courage grow.

Courage can happen to anyone. Courage doesn't require us to be the smartest, strongest, richest, or most powerful superhero on the planet. It doesn't look a certain way, sound a certain way, or worship a certain way. Courage can belong to anyone and everyone—it exists in unlimited supply. I used to believe courage could never belong to me because I wasn't charismatic. I've been thrown into plenty of challenging situations throughout my life, and I've realized that courage has nothing to do with how outgoing or extroverted you are and everything to do with your willingness to listen to that small call inside of you that tells you not to retreat. Even though fear and doubt will be screaming for attention, courage encourages you not to turn back. "Go on," courage says, "and keep going."

If you're ever forced into a legal deposition, you know about the hot seat. The hot seat is where they interrogate and rip you apart across a little table. I truly hope you never find yourself there. Being bullied for three hours by a person whose livelihood hinged on their ability to destroy me was an excruciating experience. I sat in the hot seat with my attorney on one side and Mike on the other. A stranger sat in the corner transcribing every word being spoken, and across from me sat the person who was trying gain custody of my children. I wondered how I had gotten there, why somebody like me had been chosen for this moment, this experience. As I sat at that table ferociously defending my name, my children, and my family, I realized I didn't need to be bigger or louder to be courageous, I just needed to be me—unapologetically.

Courage isn't a myth or a mystical power floating in the ether, it is real and available to all of us. Even if you don't see it, it is inside of you right now, so don't ever forget it's there. The ignition that makes your heart beat faster, courage is the whisper of hope telling you your voice will make a difference. A touch of courage feels like a hug and a push all at once. Even if you cannot see courage, it resides in you ready to burn bright. One year, in the middle of the fight, Z's school had a "Daddy-Daughter Donut Morning" around Thanksgiving. Each child decorated a pumpkin for their dad with words that described him. One of the words Z chose was "Courageful." Nobody had ever called Mike (or anybody) "courageful" before, so he asked her what it meant. She looked him right in the eye, flashed her big Z smile and replied, "It means you're fully of courage, Daddy. You're fully of courage because you protect me and keep me safe from anything bad."

Sisters, you might not know it or always feel it, but you are "courageful" too.

The morning Z looked into me and reminded me not to forget my courage ended up being one of the days I needed it the most. It was a brutal punishing court day, but because I had my courage, because I was aware of it, I wasn't afraid. Fear is life asking you to do something brave, so even if you don't quite believe you are ready, you are. Accept the invitation, step into your glory, and allow it to grow by making one hard choice at a time. Remember your courage every time you step out the door.

Chapter Eleven:
WHEN IT'S OVER

"Hey, I owe you an apology."

When I read those first words in my Instagram direct message box, I got nervous. It was sent from someone I didn't know, so I was anticipating your run-of-the-mill Internet shaming, obviously chased by some half-hearted regret. I was used to the trolling and vitriol. It had happened to me a lot, and I expect it happens to anybody who puts their life out there online for the world to see. However baseless DM tirades may be, they are hardly ever enjoyable to read, so I hadn't been bothering with them much. I adopted a very healthy practice of deleting, blocking, and never engaging with certain senders. The day I received this particular message, I was not in the mood to be bullied by yet another perfect stranger. We'd just returned from another meeting with our lawyer, and I was exhausted. We had been fighting for months and everything still seemed so uncertain. I didn't have the energy to read that I was "fake" or a bad Christian, but for some reason, I opened the DM with a strange urgency. Sensing something about this note was different, I took my hundredth deep breath of the day and started reading.

Instead of an assault, I had received a beautiful and tender-hearted admission that stuck with me for days. It began: *I've followed you for a while and I've always thought, "Lucky her. She has a nice, 'comfy' life to fall back on if anything ever goes wrong for her...."*

I gulped audibly and continued reading.

"I was so wrong to think that. I'm sorry. I know that so much of your picture I have painted myself, and that isn't right. I'm sorry for feeling jealous and mean, I don't even know you. You're a human being, you hurt like all the rest of us do, and lately, I can tell from your posts that you ARE hurting."

How did she know? I hadn't mentioned the fight on social media—I wasn't legally allowed to. I had stopped posting about the kids completely, which any mama with a social media account knows, is half the fun of having one. I'd done my best to remain positive, to spread hope and encouragement to the sisterhood that had gathered around me, but I suppose in some accidental way, I'd alluded to a struggle, some abstract, secretive pain I was going through. This sweet girl had somehow picked up on it.

The letter went on. She opened up about her own struggles: a long court battle (what are the odds?!) and a bleak future; not enough money; not enough time or space to tackle what she was facing. It was ripping her apart to the point where she couldn't sleep, eat, or take care of herself properly.

"No amount of cushion makes the pain better. I know that now, and I'm sorry for making assumptions. I'm stuck, I'm sitting here just waiting, just hoping for the next train to come and take me away from all of this. Do you ever feel stuck too?"

I started laughing, cackling actually. Mike came bounding into the room hoping I'd found a hilarious YouTube video. I don't know exactly why I found this girl's earnest message so funny. Maybe it's because I had expected a bitter rant and had been so, so wrong. Maybe it's because I'd been obsessing about portraying my life as it really was and obviously, in some ways, life was looking a heck of a lot "comfier" than it actually felt. Maybe it was the fact that I saw so much of myself in this stranger. Just a few months before, I was her—terrified, paralyzed, and stuck. After a few more minutes of reading and re-reading, I decided that my fit of laughter must have come about because of the train metaphor. Everyone loves a train metaphor, because they are simple and they make so much sense. I had spent months right where this stranger now was, waiting for the Miracle Express to toot its little horn and whisk me away to my *real* life. My real life was the place I had always been sure I was destined to go, and it was as far away from my actual current life as possible.

It had been a terrible year. We, the LeMieuxs, were completely derailed. The adoption process was disruptive, the kids were struggling and stressed, and all of us were losing sleep. It wasn't just the adoption though, it was everything else that had piled up on top of it. We had spent $125,000 on lawyers. My most trusted colleagues at work had betrayed me and left my other baby, The Shine Project, in less than shiny condition. Mike was let go from his job because he refused to pick up and move to Los Angeles while trying to save his family, and while his wife was trying to keep her company from going belly up. We were all afraid. Life was too much and it certainly didn't feel fair. For months, all I wanted to do was kick and scream and throw myself on the ground. I thought because we were hurting and in jeopardy of losing those who meant the most to us— our children—we'd be protected from any and all other challenges.

When was it all going to be over?

When was life going to begin again?

These were the two questions I asked God and myself constantly. I was so upset and livid that I gave up for a while. Everything in life was going wrong, so I resolved to stop living and simply wait until reality decided to turn right again. Opportunities came and went, and I kept waiting for my train to come barreling into view, for life to apologize for its bad behavior and start doing amazing things to make up for it. We'd get the kids (of course), a giant game show check to cover our legal fees would land in our hands miraculously, and I would be granted lifetime immunity from the stomach flu for all the vomiting I'd done since the fight began. Believing I had it all figured out, I just kicked back and kept listening for that whistle, or for some sign that the life we deserved was on its way. All the while, the life we had was passing us by.

Spoiler alert: I never did hear that whistle.

Life owes us no debt; if anything, it's the other way around. Why do we sit waiting for some sort of reward when we are actually experiencing the reward itself—this, our one life?

I am so grateful that a close mentor and confidante reached out to me during those hard, early months when I was still stubbornly waiting for the bad stuff to pass and for life to begin again. This woman was close enough to know about our battle for our kids, and in the way that all good mentors know what to do, she swooped in and dropped some serious wisdom when I needed it most:

"If you live for when it's over, you will be let down."

With those words, I realized that waiting to breathe until the ring of my doorbell did not mean having to deal with another caseworker was foolish, if not dangerous. I kept waiting to feel joy and to celebrate once we won our case—once we knew the kids would get to stay. I was waiting to feel whole and happy until I knew one hundred percent that the wholeness and happiness of our family was a certainty. But there's the truth, dear readers: Nothing is ever certain, so there is no use waiting for things to be "just so." There is no sense in waiting over living.

The upheaval in our lives had been so unexpected. On a typical boring afternoon, I got a letter that said my kids could be taken from me. It was unthinkable, and when something unthinkable happens to you in a blink of an eye, it means something unthinkable could happen again. And again. It means that the mechanics of life we thought we knew so well work differently than we thought they did. They say that life does not always go according to plan, and they are right. The revelation that life often runs its own course or at times runs off the track we set is enough to give anyone pause for reflection. But, when that pause turns into waiting, we stop living. We stay still and scared. We start to feel bitter and helpless, but we're not either. Sisters, you are powerful, beautiful, magnificent human beings and you don't need a train to take you anywhere, you can get anywhere you want to all on your own.

My mentor's words were a strong and quiet invitation.

"Ashley, stop waiting. Your life is happening right now. Go live."

And that's what I did. I ripped up my prepaid ticket to "Happy Family of Four, AZ" and started walking there myself. I relished in my kids' successes and excitements, I built valuable relationships, and I pursued meaningful work. And I did it all in the midst of the same fears, pains, and anxieties I had let stand in my way before. Along the way, I still felt pangs of despair, but I also felt happiness, hope, and peace. Because I chose to stop waiting and decided to make my own way, I arrived at my destination. If I had kept waiting, I would have missed out on some of the most beautiful moments of my family's time together. We played, traveled, and ate a lot of ice cream. Z lost her first tooth, and S learned to ride his bike. I went to sleep at night with the comfort and security of knowing I was making the most of every single second I had with my kids. Most importantly, I showed them what happens when you stop waiting for someone or something else to take you where you want to go, and you find the courage to begin the journey yourself.

I understood what the girl had written to me via Instagram. I understood what she had seen and why she had initially felt jealous. She saw me living my life fully, while she was still waiting to live her own. The image of immobility is a painful one. I'd experienced it many times and felt exactly how she did. We all tend to turn a single photograph or one brilliant-seeming moment into a storybook, but I cannot express what a dangerous instinct this is. Social media narratives especially can be misleading and disheartening. Though on a smartphone it might have looked like things had fallen perfectly into place for Mike and I, the reality was that every joy we had experienced was a direct result of choosing to live with courage. Daily, Mike and I made a choice while we struggled with the fear that our children wouldn't be ours one day.

We don't get to choose what happens around us, but we do have power over what happens inside us. We can choose to take action and start walking in the direction that calls to us. We can choose to look for love again, to take an interview for a new job, to get a divorce, or to work on a marriage. We can choose to meditate, not in the absence of fear, but in defiance of it. We dream of arriving at our next destination because we are not happy where we are. We dream about tomorrow while the sun sets on today. Sweet sister, I want you to know that you don't have to be the passenger in your own life, you can be the pathfinder. If the trek gets lonesome for you, I've known God to be an excellent travel companion.

It took me a long time to write the girl from Instagram back, but when I did, I knew exactly what to say. It was late, and I had just peeked in at the kids for the zillionth time. I could never get enough of their perfect sleeping faces. My legs were sore from chasing after them on their bikes, and my nose was sunburnt. My chest was tight because Z and I had sung "Roar" by Katy Perry all afternoon at the top of our lungs. Sitting down in my home office, I pulled up the DM I almost had not read. I felt so happy, so full, so afraid, and yet so grateful that I had stopped letting the uncertainty of the future keep me from the beauty and truth of today. I took a deep breath and typed the words that had given me the courage to walk off that dark train station platform and into the sun:

"If you live for when it's over, you will be let down. Go live."

Chapter Twelve:

THE LOSS

The timing was horrible. An emergency court hearing was scheduled for the day after I was supposed to leave town for business, and my flights were not refundable or flexible. I looked up the airline phone number and prepared to cancel, but there was really no reason for me to stay at home. The lawyers said the hearing was mostly about preparing for the weeklong final trial, which was over a month away in February. I was hesitant to send Mike to the courthouse by himself, but we weren't exactly newbies at that point. When he told me he'd be fine, I knew he would be.

Still, I hated going away. Once I became a mother, I stopped traveling for work almost completely. Mike and I were committed to providing S and Z with as much consistency, stability, and safety as possible. They were still reeling from years of chaos and uncertainty, and when either Mike or I were gone, the collective blood pressure of the house went *up, up, up*. Nobody slept well or ate well. We would mope around until our family of four was complete again. The kids thrived with routine, and I did too. I was my best self when they were next to me. If I absolutely had to go somewhere, we would all go together. I stacked events in the summer when the kids were out of school, and we made boring old work trips into the most wonderful family adventures. It might sound indulgent, but when you're used to waking up to an attack of hugs and giggles that sound like wind chimes, there's no making up for that with room service and HBO.

The one event I absolutely had to attend every year was a huge trade show in Atlanta. The success of The Shine Project hinged upon finding new retailers to carry the line. The more wholesale accounts we had, the more hardworking students we could hire and help send to college. This trade show was a critical "who's who" and a chance to meet major buyers from all across the country. That particular year—the year of the never-ending court battles—I had been asked to speak about our brand to a group of store owners, which was a massive opportunity for a "little company that could" like ours. The show fell smack dab in the middle of the school year, right after Christmas break, when the kids needed to get back to the classroom after two weeks of stuffing themselves with sugar cookies and playing Legos. I agonized over the decision, but by January of 2017, we had been in court for a year and a half. The stress was sucking everything out of all of us, extended family included. Our New Year's resolution was not to let the fight dictate the course of our lives completely, so attending this event was an act of rebellion, a show of strength, and a making good on a very important promise. Defiantly, I packed my bags.

The night before I left, Z grabbed my hand when I was tucking her in. She wouldn't let go. She begged me to stay with her, and I could tell right away that she was afraid of something bigger than the monster that lived in her closet beside her church clothes. Her beautiful brown eyes were filled with worry, and she kept grasping at me. She couldn't get close enough.

"Something feels different, mama. I do not want you to leave."
She said it over and over again while I stroked her cheek and assured
her I would be back in three quick days. Z didn't believe me though;
she was adamant that something was wrong. I stayed up with her
later than normal that night, because that's what a mama does when
her baby is upset. As I rubbed her back, she finally started to relax,
leaning back into me and twirling the ends of my hair. She told
me stories about snowmen, cats, and dance class as I soaked in
the eight-year-old wonder of her. My little girl carried joy with her
wherever she went, but she also carried a lifetime of heaviness. We
protected her and S as much as possible from the custody battle, but
kids are perceptive, and Z was an empath. The kid was more intu-
itive than anyone I'd ever met and she always, always led with her
heart. She held my face in her hands and whispered that she wished
everything would just be over.

"I know, Boo-boo," I whispered back. "Me, too."

I scooped her up in her pink pajamas and rocked her back and
forth. I stared at the ceiling and prayed for the millionth time. What
happened next was sacred, a tender mercy from heaven.

Z started to cry—a hot tear or two streaming quietly down her
cheeks—and then she broke down completely. Everyone kept telling her to stop worrying about anything other than being a kid, but
how was she to do that when she didn't know what her future held,
or where she would live, or who would take care of her? Her little
tears plopped onto the blankets, and she threw her hands up in the
air as she unloaded every frustration and fear. She was absolutely
right—nothing about this situation was fair and none of it made
sense. I didn't know how to comfort her, until I did.

I asked Z to stand up. Her shimmering salt-stained cheeks
glowed in the dark. I tried to hide my face from hers because I was
crying too. I'd been crying in the dark for eighteen months for the

exact same reasons she was crying now. I told her to put her arms out, and I placed her small baby doll's crib on top of them. She was utterly confused and perfectly adorable. After thirty seconds, her arms started to wobble, her elbows began to buckle, it was getting too heavy.

"Mama," she said. "I can't carry this anymore, it's too big."

I told her she could, that she was strong enough to keep going, and I believed in her. She crumpled her little forehead and kept holding on.

After another minute, her arms started to tremble and shake again. She moved her whole body trying not to give in, grunting like a bulldog puppy. Right before she was about to drop her arms, I lifted mine up to hold the weight. There was something divine in the room.

"There. Can you keep holding it now? Can you keep holding it now that you aren't doing it all alone?"

"Yes, Mama. I can."

"Z, life is hard. There are things that seem too heavy for us to carry all by ourselves in this world. And the truth is, sometimes they are too heavy, that's why we don't have to carry them alone. I can help you now, Dad can help you, friends and family and teachers can help you. It's important that you use your voice to speak up when you are in pain so that you don't have to go through it alone.

"But what if you're not there?" she whispered.

There it was. Our biggest fear, the thing all of us trembled under, the most unbearable weight of them all. I took the deepest, hardest breath of my life.

"Z, there may come a time when I am not around. You need to know that there's a greater strength than me, or Dad, or anyone else. This greater strength will always be with you, no matter what you are doing or where you are. This strength comes from God.

Allow Him to help you. When your arms get too heavy because life is just too hard, sweet girl, allow Him to carry it for you, and you will never be alone."

We laid back down in her little twin bed covered in stuffed animals and American Girl dolls. We were emotionally drained but covered in the most profound sense of peace. We did not yet know the weight that was coming for us, but we knew that we didn't have to carry it alone.

Motherhood had brought a thousand lessons, struggles, and moments of sweetness to me. I'm forever grateful for its humbling but heartening upward climb. That moment, as Z and I sobbed softly in the dark, was the pinnacle of my journey as her mom. That moment was the most guided and most important direction I'd ever given my daughter. I watched her tilt her chin up toward a loving God and find her comfort.

The next morning, as we drove to the airport as a family, I realized Z had been right the night before—everything felt different, something was off. When we pulled up at Departures, I didn't want to get out of the car. When I turned around to say goodbye, both kids had tears in their eyes.

Z pouted, "Mama, I feel like I am not going to see you again for a very long time."

Her sentiment was sweet and senseless. I smiled and assured her I would be home in three days. We would FaceTime every night, and their dad would probably let them eat junk food. I gave them both one last mighty hug and headed through the sliding glass doors of the airport.

Turning to them one last time, a punishing wave of loss and grief crashed down on me. It was as though someone just tapped me on the shoulder and whispered, *"Psssst! You just said goodbye to your children forever."*

I looked out through the smudgy glass to the space where the car sat idling. I wanted to run right back outside and go home with my family, but I told myself everything would be fine. It was only three days. I sat in that airport alone, frozen, and consumed by what I thought was a baseless, ridiculous fear.

I snuck back to my hotel room for a shower over lunch the next day. We had spent all morning setting up our booth, and I was mess. We had a full afternoon ahead of us, and I wanted to get back to the venue as soon as possible. I was just about to blow dry my hair when Mike called. It was the day of what our lawyer had assured us was simply a preparatory hearing.

"Ashley?" Mike's voice was stern, yet soft. "They are returning the kids to their biological family. They called a recess, everyone is going to lunch, and the caseworkers told me to go home. There's nothing left that I can do. They'll call me with final instructions once they decide what the next steps will be."

I sat down on the hotel bed, one earring in, hair wrapped in a towel, and I fell apart. Time did not just stop, it slammed on the brakes and sent me skidding into a new, unthinkable reality. I had to tell my body to breathe and ask my brain to remember how to communicate with my legs and arms. I stepped outside of myself and watched as the information sunk in. I heard myself scream, watched my body crumple onto the floor, and saw sadness begin to drown me. After what felt like an eternity but was probably only a few seconds, I zoomed out a little more. I saw Mike in Phoenix trying to remember the way home from the courthouse, his hands shaking on the wheel. I saw the kids sitting in their classrooms, unknowingly just a few hours away from stepping into their worst nightmare.

Mike called again a few minutes later, as hysterical as I've ever heard him. "They aren't going to let you see the kids before they leave, and we're not allowed to tell them what is happening," he said. "Tomorrow morning, I'm to drop them off at school and come home to pack their things. A caseworker will pick them up at the end of the day, tell them the news, and take them to a meeting place. It's all happening in less than 24 hours."

I was never going to see my children again.

I felt my soul break away from my body, unable to withstand the agony ripping through me. I was helpless and stuck on the other side of the country while a legal kidnapping was being orchestrated in an Arizona courtroom. My children were being taken from me and from the lives they knew and loved. The years of fighting, of hoping, of having faith and sending up countless prayers—the years of pushing through the anxiety and believing the brokenness that we endured would be mended—were futile. We'd been sold a package of lies, and we fed ourselves these lies so that we could survive and hang on just a little longer. It was the end of the world, the screen went black, the wind stopped. I lay on the edge of the bed clinging to an overstuffed hotel pillow with my eyes squeezed shut.

I was allowed to say goodbye in a letter—a letter—that was it. The closest my children would ever be to the safety of my arms and smell of my skin would be a piece of paper I had no way of ensuring they would even receive. How do you write a goodbye letter to your child? With everything you want them to know, feel, and remember? How do you fit a lifetime of affirmation, comfort, and encouragement onto a few slips of paper? How do you explain their coming into your lives and their leaving? I sat in the hotel and wrote, tenderly, lovingly, and so, so sorrowfully. I could have written blindly forever. I would have written into eternity to avoid reaching the end and facing the fact that our time together was over. I didn't want to say the wrong things. These letters—one to each child—would be the last tangible memory they would have of me.

After I finished, I folded the letters into envelopes. I closed my eyes as I wrote their names on the outside, trying to memorize the feeling of each stroke, curve, and corner of their name in print. Then, I talked to them one final time over video.

They were eating McDonalds and laughing. Z giggled and said, "Daddy let us have McNuggets twice today! Can you even believe that!?"

Her eyes were filled with eternal light. She was smiling so hard her nose couldn't help but wrinkle. She dunked a fry into a glob of ketchup and held it up to the camera for me to see. S picked flecks of onion off of his cheeseburger and blew me a loud kiss. I remember how happy they were that night. They kept asking how many more days until I would be back, and if I'd picked up any special presents for them. A couple of our family members popped their heads into the frame to make sure I was still alive. Mike had filled everyone in.

I sobbed as I watched my own mother take Z's face in her hands and kiss her cheeks. I watched my brother-in-law look S right in the face and say, "I love you, S. Thanks for being a great big cousin to my son."

It was as though my loved ones were giving S and Z the good-bye I couldn't, as though I was loving through them. The kids ate it all up, the French fries, and the attention and warmth surrounding them. I could hardly hold myself together. I knew what they didn't know: that all this goodness was about to be stripped away, I could not save them from the pain, and I couldn't even warn them. Crushed that very last night, I didn't talk to them for long because I wanted them to remember me smiling at them, reveling in them. I said goodbye and "I love you" to the greatest loves, the greatest joys, and the greatest blessings I have ever known.

"Goodbye, Boo-boo." It was the last time I'd call my daughter by her nickname.

"Goodbye S. Take good care of your sister while I'm gone. I love you both to the moon and back. Always and forever, to the moon and back. You will always be my little sunshines."

It was the same thing I always told them, but this time it was so different, so final. They volleyed their giggles back and forth while innocently chomping away at their special fast-food dinner.

"Love you to the moon and back, Mama!" they said in perfect unison.

Mike's face entered the screen, "I love you too," I told him. "You're the greatest dad in the whole world."

I shut the computer down and thought about the last night I had spent with Z. Her little arms had buckled under the weight of the crib. Alone in that hotel room, I got so mad. I started screaming at God that He better show up for them. *You better grab on to my little girl and my little boy so tight that they never have any doubt in You. I want that they always feel loved, safe, and protected.* I didn't know what else to do, so I found myself filling up the bathtub in this unfamiliar hotel in this lonely city. I got in and submerged myself completely underwater. I screamed as loud as I could while the water filled my nostrils and mouth, "Where are you God?! Why did you destroy my family?!"

My entire body was shaking, and I came up gasping for air. I was carrying the weight and it all was too heavy. It was too much. I prayed to God that what I promised Z just two nights before in her bedroom was right—He would never leave her, or any of us, alone. But in that moment, alone was all I felt.

Chapter Thirteen:
LETTERS

I remember every single word of the letters I sent to S and Z, even though I wrote them in a fog, in what felt like absolute madness. You will have your goodbyes in life, we all do. Some may come slowly but others will come fast, too fast. Sometimes, they are final. We do a lot of preparation for our hellos, for welcoming people into our lives. When we know someone is coming, we prepare. We get our hair done and clean the house, we're sure to fill the refrigerator with delicious treats, and we think about some things they might like to talk about. The goodbye is often less of a procession. We don't think about the words we will leave our loved ones with, or calculate how long we will hold them in our arms before they walk out the door. When somebody leaves you, whether they're moving across the country, or entering hospice care, or just going down to sleep for the night, pour as much love and joy into them as you do when you first see their face on the other side of your doorway. And if it's true for you, and you get the opportunity, say "I love you." I implore you to say it. You never know when or if you'll get another chance.

I would have given anything to be able to hold my children one last time, to kiss their beautiful caramel cheeks and feel their arms locked tight around my shoulders. The last time I saw them, I was rushing out of the car to catch my flight. I thought our separation would be three days, not forever. I may never see them again.

The letters I wrote to them in that lonesome, bright white Atlanta hotel room were the only goodbyes afforded me. It wasn't what I wanted, but I made the most of what it was. Exhausted, shattered, and shaking, I poured everything I had left—the stores of energy I'd been saving in case the world ended—into a cold computer screen that would send the biggest love letters of my life via email.

No matter how many books I publish or how many talks I give, those two letters to those two extraordinary children will be my greatest, most meaningful contributions to the world. They are only a whisper of the beautiful life we shared, and my hope is that the four years of love, teaching, safety, and home will be what they carry forward with them. When they struggle, I hope memories and the ink of those letters helps fill in the blanks. Mike, S, Z, and I made so many big memories together, but the little ones that happened in between—the nights around the dinner table, our front-row smiles at recitals, the morning prayers before school—are where the magic really happened. I couldn't jam all our years of love, learning, and devotion into one goodbye letter—it is impossible to capture such light—but I did the best I could.

I wrote Z's letter first. She had been afraid of losing us since the moment we met, as though she saw our parting in a vision the second she stepped onto our stoop at just four years old. She was always worried about something though, it was her nature. Some days she fretted about school or her room being too dark. In December, she was sure Santa Claus would get lost on his way to Phoenix. During the fight, her anxiety spiraled off the charts, as she played out different scenarios daily:

What if they put us in foster care?
What if I have to choose?
What if we never get to see each other again?
What if you forget about me?

For months, I would catch her looking out the window, forehead knotted up like tree bark. I was afraid too. My deepest hope and most constant prayer in the midst of the struggle was that she would allow herself to be happy, that she would spend her childhood years, wherever those years unfolded, just being a carefree little girl. As the people of Atlanta swirled around outside my hotel, unaffected by my pain, this is the goodbye I gave to her:

Dear Z,

What a blessing and a light you have been and are in my life. You have been my best friend, my constant source of giggles and cuddles, my sunshine, and my daughter. You have been a part of some of the most special moments in my life, sweet girl, and I thank God every day for the time He gave us to be together as a family. I know that what is happening right now is a shock to you, it is a shock to everyone because of how fast it all has happened. It is okay to express yourself, and to feel however you do because those are your feelings, and they are very important. But I also want you to know that it is okay for you to be happy. I want you to be happy more than anything else that I want in my life. Don't forget who you are, make your own space, seek your own joy, and always do what you feel is right.

I know that we were supposed to be together as a family forever. I wish that things would have turned out differently, but I'm very excited for you not to have to live in constant worry anymore about who is coming over to talk to you, or about where you are going to live, or about what questions the caseworker has for you. I'm excited for you to live your life as a little girl should, and to only have to worry about the things a little girl should, like school, dance class, how your American Girl Doll's hair looks, and if your pet has enough food :)

I want you to also know how much I will deeply miss you. With every part of my heart, I will miss you, and I will pray for you. Not a day will pass where I don't remember all of the fun and happy times we've had together. Some of my favorite moments were when you pulled your first tooth out in the car, when you learned to read and ride your bike, when you learned how to tie your own shoes on the very first day of kindergarten, and when you went to the beach for the first time. I cherish every silly dance party and every song we sang together in the car. You've taught me how to love someone so unconditionally that you'd give your life for that person. I've given my life for you Z, so you could feel safe, happy, and loved. I want you to know how loved you are, how wanted you are, how unique, kind, fun, smart, and hardworking you are. There is no one else like you. Don't lose your voice.

You are my sunshine, and you always will be.

I'll see you later, baby girl. No matter where you are, you will always be my daughter. You've asked me that many times, and I want you to be certain that will never change.

Love you more than life,

Mommy Ashley

I wrote S's letter next, recalling how when he first came to us, he was a hard-nosed, protective, and tough little guy. I remembered the way he looked at me with a severe sternness in his eyes that was so jarring to see on a face so small. He was determined not to let us or anybody else in, and I knew that as he went to live in his new home, he would go through those same turbulent emotions again. Even if he didn't want to accept this huge change, he was going to need as much love as anybody could give him. S would need as much love his heart could possibly contain. I wanted him to know he didn't need to be angry, that accepting love from his biological family would not mean he was betraying us. I wanted him to know he could and should give and receive his love freely.

It was hard to give them grace, the other family, the people who had turned our lives upside down and dragged our children through the mud. They'd been vicious to Mike and I; they had behaved like animals in the courtroom, and it was hard to imagine they'd make good or even half-decent parents. As much as it made me sick to think about them singing to S on his birthday and serving Z her extra helping of mashed potatoes at Thanksgiving, I hoped with all of my heart they would choose to do those things. I prayed they would treasure every single moment that we would mourn. Getting through to S would be hard for them. Patience would be necessary, and their love toward our cautious boy would have to be steadfast and constant if they hoped to convince him to give them a chance. I prayed that somehow through the pain and the bitterness, he would find a way to do that.

Dear S,

How did I ever get so lucky to be a part of your life? What a special boy you are. I admire you for your strength, for how protective you are over Z, for how you always pay attention to the kids who need a friend, and for your creativity. You've grown so much over the past four years, and I am so proud of you. I know that you are feeling both happy and sad right now, as you've told me that you'd feel both of those things no matter where you were going to live. It is okay to feel both of those things, just don't keep your feelings inside. It is good to talk about them and to express yourself. Always remember it's okay to feel happy and to live your life. The best part about love is that it is limitless. You can give it to as many people as you want, and you'll still have plenty leftover. Love makes your heart grow bigger so that everyone who is important to you can fit inside. You are loved by so many people, S.

I am going to miss you and Z more than I can even put into words. I think this is the hardest thing that your dad and I will ever go through, but I want you to find relief and happiness in this. You've been worrying for so long, but you don't have to worry anymore.

I'll never forget how excited you were when you learned how to read, or when you drew that person on our kitchen table (hahaha!), or when you used your birthday to get donations for veterans. I'll keep all of the pictures and cards you've drawn for me. I'll never forget when you learned how to ride your bike or the first time you beat me up South Mountain. I treasure every adventure we've taken together and am thankful that we'll get to keep those memories forever.

You're a good boy, S, you know the difference between right and wrong, and I hope that you will always choose to do what's right, no matter how hard it is.

As it says in our favorite Harry Potter book, "Don't forget to live." Take life as it is in the present, live in it, find happiness and joy and gratitude in it, no matter how tough it might get. Rely on God throughout your life, lean on your family, and remember just how much I love you. I love you with my entire heart.

I will think of you every day, my sweet boy.
I love you to the moon,
Love,
Mommy Ashley

I was updated by state workers that when S and Z were given the letters, they clung on to them for dear life. It's an image I replay in my mind—them sitting in a featureless foreign room being told the news that they were not going home to us, and then being handed the letters we wrote to them. Their tears and screams play over in my mind, while all I can do is hope those words in those letters were enough. I hope they knew we did not abandon or betray them. I hope that moment would not ruin them, but would allow them to find freedom from constant worry.

We never got the goodbye we deserved. I never got to hold these children—our children—as they learned the news and the shock of it all landed square on their little chests. I never got to answer their questions or rub their tired, aching temples as the sadness set in. Our goodbyes are such precious things. Readers, please don't forget to hold them dear. Don't forget, as you greet a person with love, to leave them with love too. Don't be afraid to linger, to give those extra hugs and say those extra few words. If you don't know what else to say, say, "I love you." And always remember, the way you choose to spend your time, your day-to-day way of being, is what matters. That is what is engrained into the hearts and minds of those you love. Love isn't a one-time action. Relationships can't be created, saved, or broken in an instant. Love is a daily commitment to pour into the hearts and lives of those around you.

As I make final edits on these chapters, it is fresh in my mind that the disappointment I experienced as an eight-year-old girl came from being smacked in the face with a softball at tryouts. My daughter, at the same age, was confronted with being torn away from the people she called her family. I do not know why life divvies out pain and hurt the way it does, but what I do know about eight-year-old little girls is that their courage is fierce, and it helps them stand back up on the field. I don't know what happened to you at age eight, or fifteen, twenty-six, or forty-two, but I do know that no matter what has been taken from you, somewhere inside of that resilient heart of yours lives a little girl. This girl wants to trust the world, find her courage, and stand back up, so let her. Write her a letter to let her know how much you love her and to give her the permission she needs to find happiness again.

Part Four:

YOUR LIGHT IS
CONSTANT

Chapter Fourteen:

WHEN *IT* STOPS YOU

T was inescapable. IT obliterated me. IT was grief.
Grief, for me, felt like being thrown into a deep hole and
buried alive. Grief is dark and suffocating, and while experiencing it, you are fearful of every muffled sound because you
can't see an inch in front of you. You don't know what's happening "up there," up there in that space where people are actually
living, where your people are living. Just when you gather the
strength to summon them, to scream for help, another shovelful
of earth lands on top of your chest and fills your mouth with dirt.
You are trapped, and every single part of you is weighed down by
something that's just too big to budge, too much to bear. You're
alone and even though you can hear voices, you can't speak to
them. Even though you can feel warmth around you, you can't
touch or hold onto it. You want to run and break free, but you
can't. So, you accept the fact you are just there, with IT. Feeling
colder and colder, losing your last bits of energy, you let your
eyelids close.

The grief of losing S and Z kept me alive enough to feel every
ounce of pain, worry, and fearful shudder, while at the same time
preventing me from feeling one ray of joy, hope, or mercy. After

the kids were taken from us, I felt buried, but aware; lonely, but surrounded; dead, but alive.

There are no road maps to tell us the right way to go after trauma hits; there are no navigational tools to warn us to take shelter before IT happens; there are no experts to tell us how many miles ahead the disaster is or how it will feel when IT bulldozes into our lives. There's no proven strategy to overcome pain and loss and no guaranteed set of daily practices to extinguish anxiety and fear. We all do the best we can with what we have. Maybe IT is addiction or anger. Maybe IT is an unhealthy relationship. Whatever IT is, if I could tell you how to make it go away, I would. For now, all I can do is share what doing my best with what I had looked like, and promise you that your best is enough. You have the power and strength to keep pressing forward through whatever your IT might be.

I'll never forget my first trip to the grocery store after the loss. We had been without the kids for about three weeks, and we hadn't had food in our cupboards for the bulk of that time. We were eating microwaved meals out of Tupperware. Our dirty dishes sat in the sink, feeding the flies. We didn't have any dish soap left, and neither one of us had enough energy to get out of the house and go to the store. One morning, when Mike was in the shower, I decided I would brave the trip. I stuck my numb feet into my flip-flops, got in the car with its painfully empty backseat, and hit the gas pedal.

I'm not sure what I expected, if I expected anything at all. A grocery store isn't exactly the type of place where emotions run wild (the fluorescent lighting works against that), but when I approached the front doors, the same doors I'd walked through with my kids, hand-in-hand, every single Saturday for years, my vision blurred. There were memories everywhere: the snack aisle where S would spend five full minutes choosing between Goldfish crackers and Teddy Grahams; the fresh flower display where Z would beg me for bouquets for all of her teachers; the produce aisle, full of clementines, baby carrots, and all of the orange-colored foods they loved. Z was in charge of opening the annoying plastic bags for me because I couldn't. I still can't.

Through the initial wave of memories, I took a deep breath and kept pushing my cart forward toward the cereal aisle. There, the boxes stared at me and everything started to spin. I got confused; I was a little girl crying over a math problem. Buying cereal, I had gotten used to grabbing the economical family size box, but now there were only two of us. Only two now. Nothing made sense. I stood there shaking in the cereal aisle like it was the frozen food section. Buying the small box of Chex was acknowledging the reality that Mike and I were alone. The family size box stood out like a lie though—to buy it would have been to stake claim to something that wasn't ours anymore.

My heart started pounding so loudly I could hear it in my ears. The lymph node on the right side of my throat swelled up to the size of a tennis ball. Dizziness came along with the instinct to grab the next person that walked by and tell them I was having a heart attack. I didn't grab anyone though, because it had happened before. I was having a panic attack—panic attacks had become a close companion of mine. I sprinted to the car and didn't set foot inside of another grocery store for over a year.

A couple of days after my showdown with the Chex, IT showed up again. I climbed out of bed on a Monday and walked into the bathroom to shower. I turned the faucet, and it groaned. There was no water, not a drop. I tried the bath, then the sink, and then our guest bathroom. Our pipes were totally dry. I called across the house to Mike and told him angrily that we needed a plumber.

"Ashley," he said gently. "Have you seen a water bill lately?"

The answer was no, I had not, because I couldn't get the mail anymore. Part of my daily routine with the kids had been taking the dog on a walk to the mailbox after school, and I was completely incapable of taking that walk without them. It was too much. I couldn't stomach the old routines or completing the patterns of everyday life without my children, without the shapes and colors that made every monotonous task so breathtakingly beautiful. Every familiar motion left me in a pile on the floor, just as it had at the grocery store. For weeks, there was no food in our house. For weeks, bills and letters and junk piled up. For weeks, life stopped.

When Mike finally unloaded our mailbox, it was filled with severely worded notices wagging their fingers at us and telling us we would lose our water, our electricity, and our credit cards. I got mad.

Didn't they know we were just trying to survive?

Couldn't they have knocked on our door and given us a warning?

We were in a world of pain so intense, nothing else around us mattered.

Didn't they know IT had stopped us?

Of course, they didn't know IT had stopped us because IT was not stopping them. When IT stops you, the rest of the world keeps on going. Looking out over Envelope Mountain on our counter, I knew if we didn't pull ourselves together, life was going to continue to spin right on by, and we might never get back into orbit. In theory, being able to shop for groceries or check the mail and pay bills on time should be simple, but those simplest tasks, after tragedy, can be the hardest. In those first small steps, you are beginning to move on and live a different life—this is an enormous task.

How do you continue to live when IT stops you? How do you agree to live this different life?

The past couple years of breathing while breathless taught me so much about the difference between honoring IT and letting IT stop you. Every month, week, and day, I practice three important steps, because IT can be very persistent. Sometimes, I have to remind myself of each step every hour just to keep functioning. Before you take in my way of coping and healing, and before you imagine what coping and healing might look like in your life, I want you to know: Sister, I'm sorry. I understand the pain, and I am just so sorry. Your story isn't over yet, so don't lose hope. It doesn't matter how long IT has stopped you, every day is a new chance to keep going, to pick up what you can, and take another step forward. No matter how long you've been at a standstill, you *can* move forward, even if it's just one small step at a time.

What to Do When IT Stops You

Acknowledge your pain. Sometimes it is easier to pretend and to say we're okay when we're not. I know it's easier to go around a mountain than to climb over it, but if we don't confront our pain we never really overcome it. Give yourself permission to not be okay, to sit at the base of the mountain with your feelings and be vulnerable. Look at your ache and respect it as the landmark it is. Acknowledging pain is healthier than running away or trying to quiet it with a substance, another day at the gym, overspending while shopping, or with releasing anger at the people we love. Wait, look, learn. If you give that mountain your attention, it will teach you the best way to climb.

When I was finally ready to go back into that grocery store, I stood outside its doors and said, "I don't like you, Safeway."

My goal was to tackle one aisle, one day at a time. When I stepped through Safeway's doors, I listened to my body, telling myself I was being brave. When my pulse started to race, I stopped and let that be enough for the day. All I bought that first trip was toothpaste and tampons, but I didn't care because I had made forward motion. I acknowledged the obstacle and celebrated my progress.

Acknowledging and honoring pain might look different for you than it did for me, and that's totally okay! It might be allowing yourself an hour to cry every day, reaching out to friends and family, seeking professional help, or journaling your heart out. When you can look at your pain, when you turn your eyes up at that mountain, it will show you where you need to go.

Don't set time limits or expectations. As humans we want to know what to expect. We like to set deadlines and goals. Without them, it feels like we're not in control, and that can be scary. Taking control of your life after IT stops you does not mean scheduling your recovery or planning every second of the next several years. It means you take it day-by-day, understanding that you must learn how to float before you can learn how to swim.

We went on a trip to Tulum, Mexico, after we lost our kids We thought maybe being somewhere faraway and totally different than home would be easier than spending time in a city full of memories. Mike took a photo of me from above. He was standing on a very tall diving board, and I was laying below in a cenote, just floating. A cenote is a natural spring in the ground that appears in the middle of nowhere. They're beautiful and are usually surrounded by the most luscious natural landscape. I remember seeing the photo afterwards and thinking I looked so free. The struggle to find peace and contentment had been merciless, and there I was, just floating. The wind would casually carry me to different areas of the cenote, and I would allow it to without trying to control the direction I was going. The girl floating in the photo contrasted starkly with the girl who had been kicking and flailing and swimming upstream for so long. I had spent nearly two years, through the fight and beyond, paddling against the current and exhausting myself in pursuit of the healing and peace I thought were waiting for me at the end of the stream. Overcoming IT though requires that you stop trying to control life's currents and instead accept them for what they are. Go with the flow, let them carry you, and trust that they'll take you where you need to go, when you need to get there.

Let life hug you. I had become so used to the high intensity existence of waking up in the morning prepared to dodge chaos and pain, forgetting to prepare to accept comfort and calm. I forgot those good things were even possible for me. As time went on, there were moments of relief, but at the same time, in some of those moments, my anxiety would come on even stronger. I had so quickly trained myself not to trust any goodness or safety from the world, never to get my hopes up too high. If I felt happiness, it was because something horrible was looming right around the corner. Sisters, I assure you that no amount of traveling, money, or success will bring healing when you live this way. For a while after the fight, I could never feel safe enough to let life hold me in its arms and embrace me. This meant too that I never had the chance to embrace life back.

I don't remember exactly why I was doing what I was doing, but I was standing at a window one day watching the world go by. When a sense of peace began to wash over me, almost immediately I started to fight the feeling away. I didn't want to invite peace in because it had let me down so many times before. Thankfully, just as quickly as the familiar internal battle began, this time it stopped. As the light shone in, I could feel it was wrapping me up in these words: "Ashley, let life hug you."

This was the invitation I needed to hear in order to step forward, to experience happiness again, and to let go of fear. When life opened its arms to me, I not only found the strength to settle inside them, but to open my arms in return. I gave up my self-sabotage, talking down to myself, and running away. This type of letting go can be a challenge, because when we've lived life in fear for long enough, our responses become instinctual, happiness becomes a threat, and pain takes over as the familiar place to hide. Now, everywhere I go I look for what I call "Life Hugs," and since I've started looking, I find them everywhere. The sun peeks out from behind the clouds. I see and hear my favorite bird. A penny flashes at me from the sidewalk. A stranger wears a beautiful smile. You miss out on all these gifts when you're running away. Life Hugs are the proof that there is good in the world, and once you begin to look around you as a daily practice, you'll find that proof is abundant.

IT looks different for all of us. For some of us, IT is grief; for others, IT is fear. Both have stopped me in my tracks, and no doubt, whatever IT is, there will be a moment when it knocks you flat on your back. In this moment, acknowledge and honor what stopped you in the past, but remember that IT isn't everything. Sisters, life keeps spinning. Don't let it spin without you.

Chapter Fifteen:

ROBBED

When somebody takes something that belongs to you and claims it as their own, it feels like a theft, a robbery, a betrayal. Such acts go against the assumptions we make about the people that live alongside us—we wonder, is everybody trying as hard as we are to be good? Are others looking out for us the way we are looking out for them? Are our ideas of right and wrong essentially the same? When you are robbed, you might lose your best jewelry or your crappy car, but the most precious thing you lose is your faith in others.

We were home when it happened. The kids had just gone to bed for the night, and Mike made me shut the back door. It was mid-October in Arizona, and the temperature had finally fallen below 100 degrees. I wanted to feel the cool air on my face; I wanted to let it flow through our little house and enjoy it. The news was on, and the anchorwoman was warning us that robberies in our area had spiked because people (like me) were leaving their doors and windows wide open. I shut the door obediently when Mike asked me to, but I laughed at him too for being such a Dad, such a protector. He always took the news *way* too seriously.

Mike and I were cuddled up on the couch nodding off when our dog started barking. I heard footsteps scraping along in the gravel, but I assumed it was the neighbors we shared a side yard with. They sometimes stayed out late. Not thinking much of it, I shut my eyes and went back to sleep in Mike's arms, but the yapping and growling continued for twenty more minutes. Suddenly, there was a strange sound at the front of the house and I could tell that somebody or something was outside, and close. I shook Mike awake, "Go check on the kids! Go! NOW!"

In my heart, I was sure I was overreacting. I really wanted to be. I told myself it was probably just a rabbit, a stray cat, or a snake (please, not a snake.) Whatever it was, if the kids were hearing it the way I was, then they were probably afraid. We'd worked so hard to make sure they felt safe and secure with us, and we weren't about to let anything jeopardize that. Mike leapt up from the couch. Our cozy 1920s bungalow was built in a circle, so he had a long lap to run to make sure everybody was snug in bed and dreaming away.

We had let Z fall asleep in our bed that night. She loved our big squishy pillows, and we loved indulging her. Sleepy and scared, Mike forgot she was in there and darted into her room instead. When he disappeared through the door, call it a mother's intuition or too much *Law & Order* but I knew something was wrong. Just as I picked up the phone and dialed 9-1-1, I heard a window slide up.

"What are you doing!?" I heard Mike yell.

A loud thud came next, followed by the shattering of glass and more footsteps. I screamed. The operator on the other end of the line was trying to get me to speak. I froze for a second, but then was frantic.

"Somebody just broke in and attacked my husband! You need to come right now! I need to get my children! There's someone in our house, and you need to come right now!"

If I looked into Z's room and saw Mike bloody on the floor, I would lose the strength that I needed to protect my kids. As I took off full tilt to grab S, I smacked right into my very much alive husband's chest. I'd never been so relieved to see him. I pulled S out of bed, and we all ran into our bedroom where Z was still asleep, snuffling and unaware of the chaos circling around her. We locked the doors and waited for the police to come. I remember sitting huddled under the covers, reading the kids a book, trying and failing to stay as calm as possible. My teeth chattered all the way through *Where the Wild Things Are*.

The cops arrived, knocking short powerful knocks on the door exactly the way they do on TV. They stood in the living room and listened to Mike tell them about the man who broke our daughter's window and started climbing in. He told them he punched the guy right in the face. Mike had never hit anybody before, and I could tell my kind-hearted, gentle husband didn't ever want to do it again. The old windowpane had shattered when the man stumbled backwards, and Mike slammed it shut. The robber fled on foot, and though the police had gotten a decent look at his face, they weren't able to catch him. He was still out there! It turns out, that when it comes to intruders, you can do a lot worse than cockroaches.

We slept at my parents' house that night and the next. Home, the place Mike and I had built tenderly together and were raising our children in—the place that held family dinners, game nights, and play dates—had been broken into. The robber didn't take anything, but in many ways, he took everything we most valued. He robbed us of our sense of safety, security, and peace.

When the time came to go back, we got the best alarm system money could buy, and the kids slept with us in the bedroom with the door locked for months. When they were ready to go back to their own beds, not a night went by where I didn't wake up in sweat-soaked panic. Every little noise—the dog's toe nails tapping on the tile, the thermostat adjusting, a car rolling by on the street—would wake me and keep me up, coiled and ready to leap into action. We wondered who the would-be-robber was, to the point where I was staying up late obsessed over his attempt.

Why did he choose our house?

What did he want?

How long had he been watching us?

Did he pick Z's window on purpose?

Does he have any idea what he's done?

Can he look at himself in the mirror?

The police never caught the man, so I never got any answers. I also never stopped worrying he would come back to finish what he had started, and ultimately, we ended up selling our house because it could never feel like home to us again. A stranger took that home from us; he had forced us out.

A few years later, in the house we'd moved in to and somehow managed to find feelings of home again, I sat in the emptiness of Z's room just trying to feel the essence of her. I ran my fingers across her pink bed sheets, one of the only items left after her room was stripped and packed up. I looked at her empty closet, her now blank walls, and the light-up heart too big to fit into the truck that delivered her belongings to their new house, wherever that was. I breathed in what was left of her in the linens until I collapsed. The rug burned my cheek, but I could hardly feel it. I tucked my legs up into my chest hoping if I made myself small enough, the pain would pass right over me. Mike and I had been robbed again, but this time, they had taken our children, our heartbeats, our everything. I asked some of the same questions I had asked the first time around:

Why us?

How long were they planning this?

Do they even care about Z and S?

Do they have any idea what they've done?

Will they ever be able to look at themselves in the mirror? Will I?

The real heartache of being robbed of what you cherish isn't in the loss of the "stuff" itself, it's in the confidence you lose in humanity, God, and yourself. Being disregarded as a human being by another human being eats away at the implicit trust we have in each other, trust that allows us to live and work together, trust that allows us to help each other and walk around each day with our hearts wide open. Once that sacred conviction, this belief in the essential goodness of the world you live in begins to fade, how do you get it back?

The fastest way to correct an imbalance in a world full of people you're not so sure about anymore is to pour your own goodness into it, to be the kind of person that you want to see. After The Loss, I sank myself into The Shine Project because I didn't know what else to do. There was no way of knowing how much helping people and witnessing the agency of others stepping up to help too would restore and grow my faith in humankind. Day-by-day, moment-by-moment, I saw the goodness I was putting out into the world reflected back at me, and I started to trust again. Yes, I had been betrayed, and yes, there was still much healing to be done, but when I took a step back and looked at the people around me, I saw more giving than taking. What a beautiful view my work offered.

Trusting God again was harder and more humbling. Trying to assess His role in what had played out in terms of the family and home Mike and I had been building with S and Z was challenging, and it hurt. I had always been certain God loved me and would protect my family, and me; but, where was he when I needed him most? What did this loss mean in terms of Him and I? After The

Loss, my faith was paper-thin and my anger, strong. Frankly, God was in the doghouse. He had a lot to prove.

In the first few months without S and Z, I spent a lot of time reliving memories of them, looking at family photos, and writing them never-to-be-mailed-or-read letters. Eventually, as I walked around in those joyful moments, I realized that God had given me much more than he had taken. My children were gone, but He had trusted me to care for them in their most fragile, vulnerable years. He chose me to be their mother when their biological family could not care for them. He chose Mike and I to give them love and safety when it was missing in their lives. He poured his goodness into me so that I could pour it into them, and I will be forever grateful He chose us for such a special, life-changing journey. I was still furious at the people who robbed us of them, and my inability to forgive tortured me. In Him though, I found peace, comfort, and resolution. I am not anybody's redeemer, He is.

People can rob us in a hundred different ways, whether they are cognizant of it or not. The one thing nobody can take from us though is our light and our ability to shine. If you're here reading this after having undergone any kind of trauma, tragedy, hardship, or unwanted intrusion, know that you are still you and nobody can take that away. Be the person you long to see in the world; be the partner, friend, or mentor you hunger for; be the goodness that tips the scales and see what happens. Open your eyes, sisters, and you'll see more people lifting each other up than pushing each other down. When you feel ready, choose to trust in the hand reaching out for you. If you get robbed again, and you may, know that it is better to live in the world as the robbed than the robber.

Chapter Sixteen:
BROKEN CAN BE FIXED

"The good thing about being broken, is that broken can be fixed."

I took a long, shaky breath. Her words on the end of the phone lifted some of the weight from my shoulders.

"I know you feel destroyed right now, but that doesn't mean you won't feel whole again one day. The return to wholeness will be slow and things will look different than they did before, but you can choose to put the pieces of your life back together in any way you want. Take as long as you need. You can build something truly wonderful, and I know that you will."

She was our favorite caseworker, the one who picked our children up from school that day and told them they were not coming back home to us. She knew the pain that covered us, because it covered her too. She had fought for us, gone to war for our family— our loss was her loss too. We cried hard together on the phone. What I would have given to reach across the country and hold her in my arms.

We were in Nashville, Tennessee, when she called, the last place I expected we would be. I drove up straight from Atlanta after hearing the news. Mike jumped on a plane straight after dropping the kids at school for the very last time. I rented a white Chevy Aveo that smelled like cigarettes from Hartsfield-Jackson airport and started driving. Having to stay focused on the interstate felt like the safest thing for me to do—I wouldn't be able to stop and crumble the way I wanted to. When Mike and I talked on the phone after he hugged S and Z goodbye, we both agreed that we couldn't go home, we couldn't be in Phoenix. The empty house with its empty bedrooms that once spilled over with laughter, love, and belonging—no, not yet. That house wasn't a home anymore, it was a memorial of a family that used to be, and we weren't ready to pay our respects. So, we picked Nashville, a brand-new city that I could get to on one tank of gas and Mike could fly to non-stop from Sky Harbor.

We spent our first night together without the kids in a dark Mexican restaurant. Tacos were the first food either of us had eaten in over thirty-six hours, and they tasted like sand. We sat beside each other because sitting across the table felt too far away, and besides, we needed to physically lean on each other just to stay upright. We cried into the salsa and wondered what we could possibly do with the giant empty space we were left with. There was nothing we could say, we were trying to figure out what to do with the rest of our lives, and neither of us knew where to begin. I kept thinking about what our caseworker had said to me.

"Broken can be fixed."

Broken can be fixed, but how? I wondered.

I had always visualized our life as centering around a big bright home, but that home had been completely leveled. How do you pick it all up? Where do you begin? You can mend a broken beam, you can replace the busted windows through which you used to look at life, but how in the world do you capture that *feeling* of home again? We would be starting from scratch, learning how to do everything all over again.

"I can't go back. I can't live there," I said.

Mike nodded and squeezed my hand.

Phoenix was an unthinkable place, even though it had always been home. There were too many memories there, too many ghosts. We spent a few minutes imagining life in different cities, and then we decided. Maybe it was out of convenience or maybe it was out exhaustion, but we looked at each other and smiled. Nashville was as good a place to start over as any. In that decision, we drew the very first lines of a new blueprint.

If you've built anything at all, whether it's an Ikea desk, a rocket ship, or an entirely new life, you know that construction doesn't often go according to plan. We *did* have to go back to Phoenix, and it was just as agonizing as we thought it would be. We needed to put our home on the market, find the courage to sell what was remaining of our children's furniture, and say goodbye to family and friends. We had to get our businesses in order and figure out where we would live and work in the strange new southern city we were going to live in. We had to find the people there who would help us and lift us up through the hardest time in our lives. We hardly even knew anyone in Nashville, but we needed friendship and fellowship so desperately. It took us five months to prepare, but once we were gone, we were gone. We packed up our Ford Explorer with everything that still mattered and drove away from the desert and everything we knew. Pulling out of our driveway marked the slowest, heaviest, most insurmountable distance of our lives, but we did it.

The first night we spent in our new home, we were welcomed by fireflies. I'd never seen them up close before. From the front porch, Oliver, our dog, and I watched little blips of light float across the darkness. Reflexively, I took a video to show Z. Fairy Land had always been our favorite game to play, and this was as close as you could get to living in the real thing.

After I took the video, a quick seventeen seconds that would have enchanted her, I realized she would never see it. It had been five months, but I couldn't stop living as though she were and her brother were right there beside me. I threw my face into my hands and wept while the strange night music of the South played around me. As I sat there in pieces on the porch with Oliver licking my tears away, I felt so lost and so unsure of what to do. I didn't know how not to be "Mom," and I didn't want to let go of my title. I closed my eyes and prayed. Life would never be the same, but I begged God to make it *something,* to make it livable again. A warm breeze swirled then and something shifted.

When I opened my eyes, the little twinkles of light were still there, zipping around joyfully in the night. They were so small compared to the enormous darkness of the Tennessee sky, but somehow, that sky wasn't able to swallow them. In fact, the darker the sky turned, the brighter they shone. For another hour, I sat there completely absorbed. Those fireflies shining was the first beautiful thing I'd been able to see since S and Z left. A light display was the perfect welcome and perfect message. I felt myself open up a little. Because I could see beauty again and could feel wonder, I knew my story wasn't over yet. The next day, in the still-strange, incredibly humid place we'd found for ourselves, I thought about the fireflies, and I knew I had it in me, somewhere, to shine bright in this darkness. I told Mike I was ready to do the work.

As my husband and I began to rebuild, we knew that the place we needed to start was with *us.* Our relationship was the foundation of everything, and even though we had done it before, I wasn't sure how we would learn to be a couple after being a family for so long. For months, we had stumbled through the motions of the day as two instead of four.

What do we make for dinner?

Do we need to set an alarm to wake up in the morning?
How much food do we buy at the grocery store?
Who do we take care of?
How do we learn to date each other again after years of Friday
nights at Chuck E. Cheese? What do we even talk about?

Mike and I were both tired of stumbling, and I didn't know how in the world we could support each other when were both so utterly broken. We didn't have the insight or the skills so, we got help and committed to learning. We went to counseling and discovered that we grieved differently: I spiraled into a significant depression and battled PTSD, while Mike's grief was quieter. I wanted to talk about our loss, I needed to talk about it, but Mike never wanted to vocalize his feelings because they felt too hard, and too big to put into words. We learned that there is no right way to grieve or to rebuild, and that it was perfectly acceptable for us to feel and act differently, so long as we were doing it side-by-side. Our needs were different, so we worked hard to meet each other where we were. We offered the support the other craved, even if it didn't make sense to us.

The realization that there was no "right way," to rebuild a life after experiencing trauma and tragedy—the discovery that there was no "secret" at all to moving forward—felt terrifying and liberating all at once. We desperately longed for a how-to guide on making new friends, participating in new conversations, and finding new hobbies, but there wasn't one. This lack of instructions, however, meant that there was no wrong way for us to do any of it. We could go in whatever direction we wanted to! If we did it wrong or poorly, we could go back and try again! Very slowly and not that consistently, we found comfort in that knowledge and started to relish the process of healing together as we began drawing plans for our future.

After our first month in Nashville, we challenged ourselves by setting a goal to experience one new thing every week. We started boxing, which we loved; we began cooking new foods, which we loved a lot less. We traveled together to prove to ourselves that we could create new memories, that we could still find beauty and joy. I'll never forget exhaustedly wobbling across the cobblestones in Europe after a 24-hour travel day toward the romance of Parisian crepes and Nutella smeared kisses. I'll never forget the time we rented the little boat and were lost in the Mediterranean Sea for an hour. I'll never forget Mike telling me graciously and gently in Germany that it was okay to buy souvenirs for the kids if it made me feel good, if it made the pain of being without them less staggering. If it made us happy and kept us healthy, all of it was okay. It took months to wrap our brain around the idea that we were going to be okay. Our happiness was different than it had been, but that didn't mean it couldn't fulfill us.

The new life and new sense of home we've built for ourselves is not exactly what we wanted. Nobody wants a family photo album with half the family missing, a closet filled with birthday gifts and souvenirs you can't stop buying, and a box of love letters you can't stop writing for people who will never receive them. Nobody wants their plans to go as catastrophically wrong as ours did, but even if they do, it doesn't mean you can't build something else that is meaningful, beautiful, and inspiring. There is always space for a new plan and always a reason to keep working and building. You can grieve, you must grieve—I do it all of the time—but grief and growth can sing in unison. There is room for joy and sadness in whatever shape life takes. Cradle your pain in your palms, but keep your hands open to accept the gifts that God is ready to give you. You deserve them and all the goodness in the world.

Think about those blueprints you drew of your life when you were little. Maybe you were going to get married, or you were going to become a famous actress or doctor, or maybe you were going to be a mother of two? Nobody's plan includes grief, depression, addiction, divorce, or sickness, but at some point we all experience a struggle that alters the lives and dreams we're busy building. Today, my life looks far different than the initial blueprints I cooked up when I was eleven. There was no suffering or pain written into my initial story, but hardships have brought me strength and have given my life such richness. Our plans don't always work out the way we think they will, but just because what you've built looks different than you thought it would, doesn't mean you can't find your home in it. Gratefully, I have.

If some unplanned something has taken you back to square one, today is a great day to break ground. You get to choose where you are headed, what you add back in to your life, and how you color your world again. Feeling okay won't come all at once. Rebuilding can be a slow, heart-breaking journey, but feelings of peace, joy, and purpose will come to you if you persevere. Broken *can* be fixed; life *can* be rebuilt.

Chapter Seventeen:
WAKING UP

It was the six-month anniversary of losing our kids. One hundred and eighty-two days had passed, and they had all seemed eerie and quiet. Mornings were calm. There were no spoons clanking against cereal bowls, no half-hearted toothbrushing sounds, no giggles. Evenings were even calmer. There was no schedule to follow, no big meal to cook, no crucial stuffed animal or blanket to find before bedtime. Life was emptier without S and Z, there was no way around it. We laughed and sang less, and everything from the pantry to our hearts was vacant. We were taking the business of starting over very seriously—we lived in a new city, we were trying new things, we were going to the therapist; but still, hundreds of miles away from the city that held our children in its arms, the echoes of family were impossible to shake.

My mom called me the morning of our six-month anniversary to check in and see how I was doing. She called me every month on this specific day, knowing it would never simply pass me by, it would leap off the calendar and pummel me. We talked about the sadness and strangeness of life, guessing how tall S must have gotten and wondering if Z would have started dance class, or if she would have chosen to play softball, like I did. We talked about the grief too; you have to talk about it because it's too big not to. And then, my mom said something I had been thinking about too.

"I wonder who else's six-month anniversary is today? I wonder what they lost and what they feel?"

We stayed silent for a moment, both going over an inventory of people we'd seen on the street.

Was it the little girl walking with her father?

Could it have been the old woman working at the checkout line?

Was it the man who walked out of the veterinarian's office with no dog following behind him?

Once you've seen loss in your own life and know the loneliness, you start to see it everywhere. You even start to look for it, hoping the person who needs to know they are not alone in all of it will look you in the eye.

"Before the kids left," she continued, "so many people were hurting and we didn't know. Now we know. Now, we're awake. Life woke us up."

Now and then, life sends something wholly unexpected our way. An event or experience that will change everything and cause us to see and feel completely differently than ever before, or ever imagined that we would, will manifest. Life could wake you when you fall in love, or when you get cancer; it could wake you when you survive a car crash, or when you bury your mother. Life woke us up when we lost our children.

Waking up is not easy, especially from such a sweet dream. Who would trade the warmth and familiarity of bed for the cold of the floor on your feet? Sleep is a safe space where we are comfortable and restful, and where our pulse slows to perfect rhythmic waves falling on the shore. In sleep, we let go of everything. I remember waking S up for school in the mornings. He would turn onto his belly, stick his beautiful face back into the pillow, and soak up every last cozy drop of the sleepy time he had left. I would call across the house to him and prod him along, and then Mike would go in, pick him up, and carry him downstairs. Puffy-eyed S never wanted to wake up. Neither did I.

Before the loss, life had been easy for Mike and I, idyllic even. Our parents loved us, and we both went to college. We loved each other desperately and found jobs we loved too. We spent far more of our lives connected to joy than to suffering, and when the children came to us, our joy was amplified by an uncountable percent. Our joy became so loud and so bright when S and Z entered the picture that it drowned out things in the world that were less joyful. Parenthood, playing our roles of Mom and Dad, came easier than we anticipated, and we relished in it. Our family felt predestined, like it had always been a part of our purpose on earth. We traveled everywhere with our children, went to birthday parties, and danced and laughed together. We had enough food to eat and enough money to pay the mortgage. We were living in a bit of a dream, though we never knew it, because in the very best dreams, everything is real.

When our dream shattered and we woke up, the world looked much different. Our eyes were wide open, and for the first time in our lives, we struggled to find joy anywhere. All we could see was suffering and brokenness, not only our own. We could see it in strangers' eyes and in the way they carried their bodies. Unspeakable pain was in foreclosure signs, roadside accidents, and angry phone calls we overheard on the sidewalk. We could feel the deflated, barely beating heart of the whole city and some days, it hurt to look outside.

At first, being awake asked too much. I remember driving on the highway one day behind a funeral procession and sobbing so hard I needed to pull over. The grief the funeral goers were feeling as they rolled slowly along in their long blinking lineup spilled over onto me, and I couldn't handle it. All I could think about was S and Z smiling and waving at me the last time we spoke, the screen going dark, and the hotel pillow I screamed into while curled fetal on the floor. Later that same day, I walked the dog past a schoolyard and locked eyes with a little girl standing all by herself while the others jumped rope and giggled in little packs. I thought about Z, the way she was always anxious about walking into her big brick school building by herself. The little girl's isolation called out to me so intensely I could barely breathe. I had to sit down right there in the middle of the sidewalk. Everywhere, there was too much loss, loneliness, and regret. I didn't want to see any of it any more. I didn't want to be awake. I went home and remained there for about a week. It took me time to figure out what I was supposed to do with the new lens I had been given to look through.

Two months went by, and I was in a parking lot near a grocery store and a nail salon. I saw an old woman struggling with a squeaky, rusty-wheeled cart piled high with groceries. It was almost 110 degrees outside, and the air was shimmering above the asphalt. She pushed her little body into the buggy as hard as she could, she cussed (if my lip reading is as good as I think it is), and her knobby knuckles went white. I watched her for a moment, feeling both her burden and my own. I knew it was too much for either of us to handle, so I began to pray quietly to myself in the car as the other shoppers ignored her, bonking their carts into one another in the hot metal corral beside me.

Why are you showing me this?

Why is there so much pain here?

Make it all of it go away. Make me feel better.

Oddly, asking these questions brought an overwhelming sense of calm. As my eyes filled up with tears that spilled over onto the steering wheel, I turned the car off, unbuckled my seatbelt, and jogged over to the struggling woman. When I approached, she looked up at me like she was afraid I was going to steal her purse, but then I smiled. I'll never forget the way she smiled back—it was as though her face muscles had to remember how to work, as though she hadn't moved them in that way in years. The woman seemed so touched and surprised just to be seen by another person. I packed up her trunk, helped her ease her body into the driver's seat, and finally, I understood: Life wakes you up because when you're asleep—comfortable with your eyes closed and resting—there is so much that you don't see.

The two most precious people in the world were taken from away me, but in that loss, I gained a deep connection to thousands of people I hadn't been able to see before. I could see people hurting now, share in that hurt with them, *and* I could do something about it. The something that I did do didn't have to be earthshattering or world changing—offering a genuine smile or helping push a full cart of groceries across a parking lot had value. I couldn't erase my pain or anyone else's entirely, but I could make it easier to bear for a few moments. I could take action to make suffering less solitary.

Pain was what woke Mike and I up and, sister, when pain wakes you up, it doesn't exactly come through your window like a sweet ray of sunshine. Pain is a bucket of ice-cold water on your head. When you open your eyes, expect it to hurt, expect to be startled by what you see, and expect your heart and mind to run circles around each other. But once you are awake, expect to feel a call so strong and certain to get your butt out of bed and *DO*. As grief continued to make space for growth, my entire family—Mike, of course, too—felt the call.

I can't tell you the number of times I've heard from friends that Mike had dinner sent over to them when they were sick, or that he showed up on their door step with treats at the exact moment they needed to be reminded they weren't alone. Mike wouldn't even tell me about his random acts of kindness, he would simply do them. I married a man who shows up for people in the way he hopes people would show up for him. If I try to praise him for being a good man, he shrugs it off and tells me he is simply paying attention to his feelings, and if somebody is on his mind, he figures it's for a reason. Whether it's the twenty-year-old special needs boy we go to church with calling him five times a day just to talk, or the kids' former school teachers who he brings flowers to when whenever we're in Phoenix, Mike doesn't just see people, he reaches out for them. Watching the man I love wake up and channel his own heartache into healing, watching him pour pure, unselfish love into those who need it, is inspiring.

The funny thing about being forced to wake up the way Mike and I were, or in any way, is that even though nobody likes the process, once you are in the thick of it, your eyes, heart, and soul do adjust. Once that initial jolt of agony begins to subside, you don't want to go back to sleep, and you can't. Once S finally rolled his way out of bed on Monday mornings, he was full of energy, passion, and joy. Our magical little boy took in all the things a day could throw at him with a smile on his face. He ran full tilt wherever he was going and asked a minimum of five questions a minute about space, animals, and the world. He was so awake, so alive, and so present. At the end of the day when we started our bedtime routine—dim the lights, put on the PJs, brush the teeth, and drink some water—the boy we could hardly get out of bed in the morning would be horrified by the idea of getting back in it. He would look at me and say, "No, Mama, I'm too awake. I don't want to go back to sleep. Not ever."

How wise he was. I don't want to go back to sleep either.

I miss my children every single nanosecond of every single day. Sometimes, the pain is quiet and other times, it screams as loudly as it did the very last time I saw their greasy French fry-eating faces and told them goodnight. However heavily that pain has weighed on my spirit, it has lifted my soul with equal profundity. Loss has led me down the most humbling, inspiring, and life-changing path. Waking up to the opportunity to get to know love and loss so intimately has been my greatest privilege. It has made me a better human being.

Sisters, before you stand up every morning, you wake up, you open your eyes. Most of the time you wake up because your phone alarm is blaring that annoying sound, and you want to throw it against the wall, but if our little devices didn't scream at us, we'd be late for work, we'd miss dropping our kids off at school on time, we would not make the important flight, or we would forego our gym sessions that empower us to be strong. If we chose to ignore the wake-up call, we'd miss so many of the beautiful things the world has been dying to show to us. When the alarm sounds, listen to it. Let life wake you, even if it's scary, even if it hurts. Experience the deeper connection, fill your cup, help another person fill theirs, keep your heart wide open, wake up, stand up, and DO. Trust me, afterwards you'll never want to go back to sleep again.

Chapter Eighteen:
PERMISSION TO SHINE

I f only we could pretend that what follows never happened and could bury it under a pleasant symmetrical story of learning. In this part of the story, I get lost. Of course, I could skip over whatever unpleasant truth I want to—that's one of the perks of being an author. But after all these chapters, it wouldn't be fair to anyone to paint a less-than-complete picture. I know there are parts of your story you wish you could omit too, but let's not do that anymore. Let's tell the truth. Let's honor the walks we have taken through the darkness, so that we can fully understand how it is we came to shine.

People often tell me sweet, encouraging things about my children:

"Don't lose hope!"

"They miss you as much as you miss them."

"Don't worry, they'll never forget your love. They'll find you again."

When this happens, I normally thank them and tell them how touched I am to have their support, because I am touched, deeply. What I don't tell them is that one of my children already did find me and it was devastating.

When the phone call came, I went numb. It had been nearly a year since the kids were taken from us, a year I had spent searching for answers and trying to keep my head above water. For twelve months, I was literally pinching my own skin just to prove to myself I was alive. My PTSD controlled everything, changing my relationship to everyday tasks like grocery shopping, getting the mail, and receiving phone calls. Whenever I received a call from an unknown number, I held my breath—unfamiliar digits took me straight back to the attorneys, state workers, and other bearers of bad news who had kept my phone ringing off the hook for all of 2016. Paradoxically, in the pain and panic of seeing a strange number, there was also the hope that maybe one day, it would be S or Z on the line. Maybe one day they would find a way to call us and we wouldn't have to go through life without each other. I fantasized about hearing Z's musical voice; I dreamt S would call just to tell me what he somehow knew I had been wondering about every single day from a few hundred miles away: *Yes, they were happy and healthy and everything was okay.*

When they were living with us, we stayed constantly connected to remind our two kids that we would always, forever and a day, be there for them. We got them walkie-talkie wristwatches that linked directly to our phones, and they would call us just to say "hi" or "I love you," or to invite us on very important secret agent missions. Z would call us from her room with absolutely nothing to say, just wanting to know we were still close by. The walkie-talkies weren't enough though—S and Z wanted a backup plan, another path that would take them to Mom and Dad. One of the first things we worked on as a family was making sure that they memorized my phone number. Anytime they needed me, I could be right there.

"I promise, this will be my phone number forever and always, so any time you need me, all you have to do is press these seven numbers and you will reach me!"

They nodded their little heads.

I never did change the number, and I never will.

I was standing in the kitchen when the call came in. My phone blinked up at me from the counter. I held my breath—the right area code, the right time of day.

Don't get ahead of yourself, I warned my heart, which was doing cartwheels under my ribs. *It's probably another telemarketer.* One had gotten through to me a week before and had sent my cartwheeling heart straight to the ground.

When I answered this time though, it wasn't a stranger named Melissa trying to sell me new fixtures for my office, it was one of my children. It was a voice I'd been dreaming of hearing every minute since the last time it danced into my ears.

"Hi, B@#$%. I wish that you were dead."

The words knocked me backwards into the sink.

The words didn't make sense.

That statement had come from a little human I had raised, one I had nurtured, loved, and taught about the planets in the solar system. For the next couple of minutes, I did nothing but listen. Hate-filled language, damning lies, words I couldn't even imagine that my child (or any child) had even heard before flew from the sweet little mouth that used to kiss me goodnight. My child hated me. It was the most terrible waking dream I had experienced; it was worse than the court room; it worse than saying goodbye. I put my hand to my lips and stayed silent as untruth after untruth was repeated by a scared, very confused kid who had been through unthinkable pain, a pain that we shared. My hands were trembling, but I couldn't put the phone down. What I heard even louder than the yelling, cursing, and hating was a shaky broken voice, a tender, tortured spirit who needed Mom. This child needed a safe place to let the anger and pain breathe. I allowed myself to become a punching bag, and when the punching was done, and the little voice panted breathlessly on the other end, I replied.

"I am so happy to hear your voice. I have waited for this phone call for what feels like forever. I know you're upset and I know you're angry, but I am just so happy to hear from you. I want to remind you of a few things: The first one is that I love you. Your dad and I love you and we always will, no matter what you say to us. There is nothing on planet Earth you could ever do that would make us stop loving you. I need you to know that. We will always be here, whether it's now or when you're fifty. We will be here, loving you, and waiting for you every second of every day."

I spoke love and truth into my child. I held tight to the memories and to the hundreds of stories we'd read under the covers with the flashlight, the Jack-O-Lantern we named "Smooky," and the time we got in trouble for pushing our cart too fast in Target. The best way we can help our loved ones as they struggle to see us and see themselves, is to be a beacon. We must try not to let their darkness overtake us too. It's a big job and sometimes, it feels like an impossible one.

My child grew quieter, and I pressed on as the space to speak grew wider. I let love and understanding flow over my own hurt and I packed as much affirmation into those precious moments as I possibly could, knowing I might not ever have another chance. The last words my whole world, my soulmate, my lost-in-the-dark child said to me were, "I never want to speak to you again in my entire life."

"Sweetheart," I began, but the call ended. It was too late.

The exchange hit me like a nine iron. My child wished I were dead. Of course, they were angry—we had promised them over and over again we would always be there for them, and we weren't anymore. We had been denied contact privileges. We promised S and Z we would protect them from the exact situation they now found themselves in. We failed them. Trust was broken and they felt abandoned by us. I had broken these children, when my job had been to make them whole. It was all my fault. Up until this point, I had lived with a hope that one day we would be reunited and the feelings of love and peace we tried our best to give to them early on would endure and carry them back to us. With that call, I realized those feelings were gone. Our child hated me.

With the dial tone still ringing in my ear, hope died. My light was snuffed out. I hated myself too.

I spent the night feeling numb. Mike brought me soup and tried to talk to me, but I had nothing to say to him. I couldn't even explain what had happened, it was too painful, too unreal. I wanted everything to be undone, the wonderful memories of holding my little ones tight, the adventures, the kitchen dance parties, and the tenderness of pulling the big blankets up to their little chins, I wanted it gone. All of it. No sweet memory, no amount of joy or love in my heart was worth the sadness it had brought to theirs. I curled into a ball on the couch and wept. What kind of mother lets this happen to her children?

What do you do when everything goes dark? What do you do when you can no longer see yourself and no longer know your value in the world?

After the phone call, I didn't feel worthy of love, acceptance, or forgiveness. I had failed my children, and that failure was all that I could see. I blamed myself for saying that initial spontaneous big "Yes!" to pursue adoption at age twenty-five. I felt naïve and foolish for believing that our story could be a happy one. I made reckless promises I couldn't keep and because of that, my children, the little people whose happiness and health were still my number one priority in life, were irreparably damaged. That night, I tossed and turned, replaying the phone call over and over again and letting the words sink in until I saw myself as nothing but a monster.

I woke up the next morning, groggy and miserable. My face hurt and my eyes stung. When I looked in the bathroom mirror, I saw a confused little girl whose face spoke of nothing but exhaustion, heartache, and worry. Someone I didn't like had taken the place of the girl I loved and used to be. I thought about the truth and love I had poured into my child over the phone as they berated me. I thought about the light I still heard in them, the undeniable goodness that no amount of hatred could squash. Why then couldn't I see that same light in myself? Staring at the ugliness that I was, picking my skin and inviting every vile, self-loathing thought to settle in my brain, I screamed and cried and shook furiously. And then, I stopped.

Sisters, if you're trying to find yourself, don't go looking in the mirror. You owe it to yourself to look deeper and further. Give yourself permission to shine.

I went into our bedroom and pulled out a box of photos. What I saw in image after image was so different than what I'd seen only minutes before in the bathroom. There we were on one of our family adventures, with our arms linked together and our faces glowing as we stood at the edge of Lake Louise and gazed out over the bright blue glacier water. There we were at Disney, Z and S eating churros the size of Frisbees and laughing about Mike's goofy ears. There we were at home, sitting next to each other stealing kisses and tickles on the couch. In those photographs, I saw a clearer reflection of who I was: I was a strong, loving woman, a mother who adored her children and gave everything she had to her family. I saw someone shining beautifully and brightly, someone I loved dearly. I saw my children clearly too—on their joyful, innocent faces I saw that they knew they were loved wildly. The kid that yelled at me on the phone was also the one who wrapped their arms around me at the Christmas tree farm and said, "You're my favorite present ever." What this child had sneered at me over the phone wasn't coming from a place of truth, it was coming from pain and fear.

Self-love is a skill that takes patience and must be practiced. It doesn't come to you by simply looking at old photographs and deciding that because you smiled for the camera at Disney in 2013, you can access joy anytime you put your mouse ears on. For me, the day after the call was just the beginning of my mission to look deeper. The day after the call, I gave myself permission to seek happiness. Little by little, I gave myself permission for all sorts of things, permission to accept love from my husband, to feel pretty again, to take time to develop myself, to seek help in therapy, to take a break from work, and to enjoy food and rest. I gave myself permission to cry when I was sad and laugh when I was happy. I allowed myself to experience all those things because I truly deserved them. You deserve a full life, and so do my precious children.

I hope they call again. Like I said, my number is still the same. I hope they know that our love for them is limitless and one day, it will be that incredible, boundless love that reunites us. Even more so, I hope that my children give themselves permission to find joy in their lives despite the sorrow they have walked through. I hope they learn they are worthy, and that they are in possession of the most breathtaking, glorious light. I hope they know that even in the darkness, hundreds of miles and almost two years apart now, I can still see them shining. I always will.

Chapter Nineteen:
CASTLE VIEWS

Spending our first Christmas without the kids was unfathomable. Mike and I had clung to each other over Easter weekend, barely acknowledged Halloween, and while we weren't feeling terribly thankful during Thanksgiving, we made it through by the skin of our teeth. Christmas felt different though, more impossible. It had been S and Z's favorite holiday, and they had immediately eaten up every festive tradition we built for them, from the wacky family Christmas card to the giant plastic snowman we stuck in the middle of our desert lawn and kept there until Valentine's Day.

Our first year without them, as soon as the rolls of red and green wrapping paper begin to encroach on Halloween candy in the store, I began dreading it. At the same time though, a dose of holiday cheer was exactly what Mike and I needed. We were starving for some familiar brand of easily accessible, pre-packaged joy. Whatever reprieve we could get from the pain, despair, and desperation we had been living with for eleven months was welcome. I just didn't have any idea how we would, or could find it.

Every time I sat down early that December, my brain filled with painful questions:

Do we hang up two stockings or four?

Who will put the star on the top of the tree if Z isn't here sitting on Mike's shoulders?

Will Santa show up at their new home this year, or is this the year they figure out "he" was really "us" the whole time?

How do we send out our annual Christmas photo with only the two of us on it? What do we say?

Can we use the old one everyone already has?

No answer felt right, and instead of taking on the impossible task of trying to find peace, I decided Mike and I should just run away. The more I thought about it, the better the wild idea seemed—running away could be a new tradition for just the two of us, a tradition that conveniently spared us the pain of showing up at family holiday parties with half of our family missing. Perhaps somewhere out there, faraway from this empty-of-giggles and anticipation reality, there was a healing balm to soothe us through our first December 25th without our children.

I was afraid to bring the idea up with Mike. He was a madman about the holidays, a real Clark Griswold-type, and he would be skeptical about leaving town. Knowing it was going to be a tough sell, I did what any logical wife would do, I waited until he fell asleep and booked non-refundable tickets. I spent hours in the dark quietly researching the most festive, cheerful, and snowiest places on Earth. I wanted "CHRISTMAS!!!!" not just Christmas. I wanted to go somewhere that the gingerbread dial would be turned up to 11 at all times.

When he woke up the next morning, I had the answer.

"We're going to Germany!" I screamed.

Mike had never heard me say the word "Germany" before, so he was a little stunned (and a little sleepy). I started in on my pitch right away, telling him it would be a treat-eating, small-town adventuring, Christmas Market shopping, castle-viewing, Bavarian meat-devouring German Christmas Miracle Vacation. He raised his eyebrows and looked nervous, as if to say, "But we're from the desert." It was true—ice, snow, jet lag, and hand warmers weren't exactly in our blood and historically, we hadn't functioned very well in the cold (thanks, 120-degree Arizona summers). The more I talked, the more suspicious of the whole thing Mike became. He mentioned the words "Fiji" and "coconut drink" more than once. I was persistent though: No, it *had* to be Germany. I promised I'd find all the right gear for us to wear even though I had no idea where to buy mittens in Nashville. "C'mon," I told him. "We'll be spending Christmas Eve in the town where Silent Night was first written and performed."

I saved the jewel in the fantasy-Christmas crown for last: Just as I could see him warming up to daily bratwurst and potatoes, I showed him Neuschwanstein Castle.

Neuschwanstein Castle is a 19th-century Romanesque Revival palace that sits on a hill overlooking the village of Hohenschwan-gau. Mike's guess on pronouncing any of this was as good as mine, but we didn't need to know how to pronounce a single word of German to understand that this structure was one of the most breathtaking we'd ever seen. There was something magical about it, so magical that a man you might know named Walt Disney used it as the inspiration for the iconic Cinderella's castle. If this castle was good enough for Walt, it would be grand enough for us.

We spent a long time looking at photos and counting turrets. Our favorite shots had been taken from farther away, so the castle could be seen in its entirety. We wondered where we'd have to drive to see it from that exact vantage point, and before long we had walking directions to the exact spot on the exact bridge where the photo was taken. It was done deal. To this day, I'm not sure what initially drew me to that castle—maybe it was the majesty of staring up at something that had withstood hundreds of years when we had barely survived the past eleven months, or maybe it was the strange hopefulness of something foreign and fantastical that made us feel new again—but Mike finally agreed Germany was the place for us. We had a plan, we prepared, we were off!

It wasn't the smoothest journey, and I probably won't pursue a career as a travel agent anytime soon. I kept my promise about keeping us warm by ordering an insane amount of hand and feet warmers. How could I have known they would set off every single airport security alarm, causing our luggage to get lost? I booked us a red-eye flight, thinking we could sleep through it and quickly adjust to local time. How could I have forgotten how uncomfortable, squishy, and awkward it is to sleep in coach? Mike and I were awake the entire duration of the ten-hour flight to Munich. We landed around noon local time and walked straight into a German sensory explosion. An accordion player was performing in the terminal and people were dancing around in circles drinking Kolsch. It was a lot to take in, and we weren't exactly chomping at the bit to jump into our lederhosen. Mike smiled at me and shrugged. We had been awake for a full twenty-four hours; we hadn't stayed up like that since we lost S and Z.

The plan was to go straight from the airport to Neuschwanstein, which we still couldn't say right. It was romantic and illogical, but we wanted to see the thing we'd traveled so far to see as soon as possible. The castle was over two hours away by rental car ("Surprise, Mike. You're driving!"), and our *auto* was ready for us. Our bodies and brains needed rest and probably would have settled for a nap right in the Hertz lobby, but we couldn't rest. We had a castle to see.

How we stayed awake, we'll never know. We rolled down the windows and let the freezing temperatures force our eyes open. I was so terrified Mike would fall asleep at the wheel, I wouldn't even let him use the hand warmers. Our teeth chattered as we drove up into the Alps, and the cold seemed to get even colder the higher we climbed. Our heads ached, our brains were foggy, and we were hangry (you know, the anger that comes from being hungry), but we kept going. After a seemingly endless upward climb, we pulled into the perfect gingerbread house village.

"Welcome to Hohenschwangau!"

Before we noticed anything else in the village, there was Neuschwanstein. The castle sat on the hill in full view as we rounded a mountain corner. It was more than a castle though, it was a welcome beacon, a sign that we were right where we needed to be. I was overcome by peace, happiness, grief, joy, and purpose. Seeing those turrets we had counted in photos, we felt renewed. Part of us had given up on magic, part of us was resigned to spending our lives without it, but there it was right in front of us. As the green that blanketed the hillside began to shapeshift into a forest of tall pine trees, I squeezed Mike's hand. I was so thankful that instead of giving up, we said "Yes!" to this adventure.

"Ashley!" Mike yelled.

He was pointing to a stand where a line of horse-drawn carriages stood. The horses were stamping their hooves on the cobblestones and shaking their manes. Normally, we would have loved the challenge of hiking up the hill in front of us, but that day we took on a challenge that had eluded us for months—we let ourselves fall in love again with life, after it had hurt us so badly. We climbed right into a carriage cab and cuddled close under a wool blanket while our Bavarian driver sang carols in German. Steam rose from the horses' nostrils and flew back at us through the frigid air. As they broke into a trot, I started to feel panic. Why was my heart was racing? As the ascent continued, I realized I wasn't panicking at all, I was excited. I had not felt excitement in so long.

We arrived at the old stone base of Neuschwanstein, *our* castle. It was magical. In the depths of the despair we had been living in, we forgot there were things to marvel at all around us.

Standing right next to the castle was phenomenal, but sometimes, being too close to something prevents you from seeing the way it fits into the world and changes the landscape around it. Since that first day of planning our trip, we'd been utterly enamored by the photo taken from the faraway bridge. Ultimately, it was that photo that had brought us all the way across the ocean. I pulled out my notes, found the trailhead, and we began walking toward the vantage point we'd been dreaming of looking out from.

We crunched through the snow, over slick frosty pebbles, and up to a heavy gate. The path was barricaded, closed down by icy conditions. There was no other way to the bridge, and with a single *Achtung!* sign, our dream literally froze. In an instant, after twenty-eight hours of no sleep, lost luggage, "hanger," and a poor footwear choice for castle hiking, frustration rose up in me. I yelled at Mike, "Why can't anything ever be easy?! WHY?!"

My voice echoed out into the mountains. I almost started crying, but mid-tantrum I noticed people were going under the barricade to start the hike up anyway. Mike and I glanced at each other, nodded in tandem, and silently agreed that we weren't going to let a half-hearted fence stop us from the experience we wanted. We climbed under the gate, feeling brave, rebellious, and as full of gumption as the others.

The hike up was pure dramedy. Mike's Converse sneakers weren't made for scaling a 65-degree slope covered in slippery, wet, compounded ice. He slid around, grabbing onto foliage, snow banks, and me, while I lifted my too-heavy boots and begged the path to show some empathy to two American kids on a quest for a castle. At one point, a side rail finally appeared. As quickly as we threw ourselves on it, we threw ourselves off it. About four inches above the handhold, a long line of barbed wire ran all the way up the hill. Now, Mike looked like he was going to cry.

Of course, I thought, *it makes perfect sense to have barbed wire on a handrail.*

Wire or no wire, we needed that rail and were not going to let the mountain win. We moved slowly and carefully behind the other crazy tourists, knowing if any of us moved our hands too high or slipped and lost control, we'd be spending Christmas in a German hospital. Our herd stayed vigilant and hyper-focused, puffing hot breath into the air and taking teeny tiny sideways steps. We lost a few in our gang along the way. They went sliding downhill on their butts and shaking their heads, but we were determined.

When we finally made it to the road at the halfway point, we rested for a minute. We were hunched over and gasping, but we were smiling too. I couldn't believe it, we really were making this love-lorn pilgrimage to the castle that would make everything better. I looked over at Mike grinning in his sopping wet sneakers. In that moment, I loved him and his terrible shoes so much I could hardly bear it. The next part of the path was even more treacherous, but after climbing through another barricade and clinging desperately to another rickety handrail, in two hours we made it to the bridge where the photo we had built this Christmas dream around was taken.

As soon as we stepped out onto the bridge, we realized why it had been closed. There were holes everywhere and the wood was rotting. The bridge was unsafe, but we took a few steps. We had to. I exhaled, "Mike. Look."

She was right in front of us, and she was glorious. She was the castle of our dreams. Standing in her shadow, I felt part princess, part Indiana Jones. We had a front row seat to Neuschwanstein, which was everything we had hoped it would be. A waterfall rushed below us, sending clear blue water down the mountain. Fresh snow sat on the castle turrets like sugar icing. The air glimmered with snowflakes so small and sparkly it looked like Tennessee fireflies had made the trip with us. I spent a long time looking at the castle, watching the sun reflect off of her stone and glimmer at me. Finally, I understood.

"This. This is it. This is why things can't always be easy. Because the reward is so great sometimes, we just need to fight for it."

Mike smiled at me, and we listened to the waterfall rumbling underneath us.

On the way back down the forbidden trail, we once again faced plenty of dramedy, but it felt different than it did on the way up. We passed people who were on the start of their hike, wide-eyed and scared like we had been.

"Keep going," I would say. "It's hard to get up this stretch, but the castle views are worth it."

Of course, not everyone could have known what I was saying, but I said it anyway, hoping the look on my face was enough of a translation. Something changed in me that day: I had learned to savor the climb. The climb is where the hard work happens, where you confront every fear, pain, and anxiety. The climb is where ask yourself every few steps, "Is it really worth it?" and you must answer back, "Yes!"

Working through every barrier, doubt, and moment of exhaustion is what makes the viewpoint on the summit at the broken bridge so astoundingly beautiful.

Sweet readers, I'm not suggesting you follow my lead and break into a German forest or stand on a condemned wooden overpass—what I am saying is that life is hard, dreams are out of reach, and goals are often placed behind barriers. Sometimes we even put those barriers in place ourselves. Tighten your shoes, sisters, and keep climbing. Don't stop at the first, tenth, or twentieth setback. Fight to the end for those castle views or for whatever motivates you most. Your life's best scenes are waiting for you, they are ready for you, and they are worth the journey.

Our German Christmas retreat was one of the best trips Mike and I have ever had. We laughed, we cried, we listened to polka music. We felt lonesome in some moments, and so connected in others. Had we stuck to what was familiar, known, or expected— had we chosen to stay behind the barriers set out in our path— we would have missed out on something magical. We would have missed out on what we needed most.

I don't know what our children did that Christmas. I don't know if Santa came for them, or if they were surrounded by family or friends. Did they get stockings? Were they told how loved they are? I don't know the answers to any of the questions that bombarded me that first holiday, and to be honest, they'll always be unanswered. But I do know that if I see S and Z again, I can tell them what happened when Mama chose to keep climbing, and I can tell them when things get tough, they can choose to keep climbing too. I can tell them about magic because I've seen it, and maybe one day we can all stand together on the broken bridge that looks out over Neuschwanstein Castle.

Just because your path has been blocked, changed, or completely obliterated doesn't mean there isn't something beautiful waiting at the end for you. Trust that there is something to be gained on every journey upward. Certain stretches might be hard, but I promise the castle views are worth it.

Chapter Twenty:
STAND UP AND SHINE

N ow that this book is coming to a close, I feel it's time to get blunt. If I don't, I'll be doing a pretty big disservice to you, and I love you far too much to let that happen. Here goes:

Going to visit a castle in Europe does not make everything better.

Learning to box does not make everything better.

Having a perfect body or a perfect partner, or moving to a new house in a new city will not make everything better.

Healing isn't a moment; it's movement.

Healing is work that is constant. At times, it takes daily, hourly, and moment-by-moment commitment. The work is hard and unforgiving, but it is such good work. Dear reader, my dear friend, I know you may be hurting. I know you may feel weak. I know tomorrow somehow seems so much easier and brighter than today does, but you have a lot of work ahead, and you are the only person who can do it. The time to start your journey onward—to stand up and shine—is right NOW.

Thousands of women have followed my story and written to me. Their words have been the most humbling, affirming, and encouraging gift. Right when I needed it, right when I was stumbling backwards, I had an incredible community of women lifting me up and telling me to keep on going. It has been my greatest privilege to try and do the same for them. Still, daily, there is one question that keeps coming up in my inbox:

"Ashley, I'm stuck. How do I get unstuck? How do I find the purpose that will keep me going?"

Readers, when you're all the way down in that awful place, the place we all find ourselves in when life gets to be too much, you have to believe in yourself. Believe relentlessly and aggressively. It's okay if you don't have the energy to believe right now, because believing in yourself takes time and work. We cannot be "on task" 24/7, especially after trauma, loss, or heartbreak.

I've found unearthing our will to move on is less about uncovering our purpose and more about uncovering our power. You know your power is in there, don't you? You can feel it. You might use it daily, or you might fight against it because you don't think it's strong enough or good enough. Don't deny it though, it *is* your beating heart and all of the wonderful things you can do with it—with love. You might not always acknowledge your light and strength, but you are mighty, and it shows when you do something challenging or unusual. When you befriend a stranger, when you love yourself, when you are kind, and even when you are angry, your light never extinguishes. If you can see even a flicker of it, and can acknowledge the sheer life force in you, you can let it propel you to seek a purpose, seek healing, and seek joy. The question I would like to see from more readers, more of my sisters, is this:

"I'm ready. Where do I begin?"

I've shared my story with you, but I'd like to share my strategy too. This isn't me showing you what your purpose is, it's about you learning that you have the power to go out and find it on your own. It's about showing you that you can stand up and shine; in fact, you are shining right now as you read these words. I didn't always believe in myself, and I still don't some days, but I know that I am powerful enough to do the work and move forward—even if some days I have to tell myself to simply make it through the day. There is no perfect plan and there are no universal rules, but these are the first steps I take whenever I feel stuck. When I'm ready to do the work of moving forward, this is where I begin:

Stand Up and Shine: The First Steps
1. You Are Not Stuck. You Are Just Standing Still.

Many of us struggle with self-doubt. I know this is true because of the thousands of stories women have told me, and because of the stories I've told myself. Some of you reading this may have even written me emails, sent me messages, or cried with me in person because you didn't feel worthy of the beautiful life you deserve. Why is it that the second we dream a big dream or think about what we want in our lives, we let the gravity of ambition stop us in our tracks?

We freeze when we think of all of the reasons the life we want could never be ours. We stand looking up at the dream instead of walking towards it. Most of the time though, there is no wall, no barrier. The only thing standing in our way is that icky self-doubt tricking us into feeling as though we've waded into mud. When I find myself standing still, I take ownership of that big dream—whatever it is—before I even get there. I say to myself, "Yes, you can."

Go on, try it. Say "Yes, you can," out loud.

- Now try this:
- Yes, you can be happy.
- Yes, you can do hard things.
- Yes, you deserve to be loved.
- Yes, you are strong enough to stand up for what's right.
- Yes, you can make money.

- Yes, you can travel.
- Yes, you can be a good mother/wife/friend/sister/daughter.
- Yes, you can have a positive impact.
- Yes, you CAN.

Shout this last mantra out: Yes, you CAN. Write it down. Stick it on your mirror. Put it on your car dashboard. Make it your screensaver at work. The next time you feel stuck, look at these words and commit to them. Take ownership of your dream before self-doubt takes ownership of you. Put your hand on your chest, feel that beating heart that is your life in forward motion, and say out loud:

"Yes, I CAN, because I AM."

Maybe you're not stuck. Maybe you're just standing still. You are far too talented and lovely to spend any time doubting yourself. You can do it! It's time to get to work.

2. IT isn't a Void; IT is a Usable Space. Fill it with Light and Positivity.

When I lost my kids, a huge chunk of my heart went with them. I felt so empty, shattered, and lost. I tried to fill the void with Netflix and social media. I thought if I could escape into someone else's life, then maybe I wouldn't have to feel the heavy reality of my own. The more time I spent away from my own life though, the emptier it felt to return to at the end of the day.

Whether it's cotton candy, vodka, or shopping sprees, we all try to fill ourselves up when we're empty. Some of what we reach out for is convenient, but not always healthy. New shoes are pretty and chocolate is divine, but neither will keep us feeling full for long. I ask you to stop thinking of emptiness as a void to be filled and instead imagine it as a space to discover and build on.

When we feel broken, when we have lost something that was a great part of us, we have a unique opportunity to choose what we allow back into the space that's left behind. Every time you feel the urge to fill a loss with social media, or shopping, or shutting people out, acknowledge what you are doing. Ask yourself if you are honoring the beautiful space you've been given and have known. If you aren't being good to yourself or others in the moment, recommit to filling the gap with something different. When I'm feeling tempted and am reaching for something that I know isn't good for me, I do one of these things instead:

- Send a text to a friend to brighten their day
- Write a handwritten note to encourage someone
- Make a phone call just to catch up
- Go for a walk
- Spend more time with family
- Plant a flower
- Read a chapter in a book
- Write a journal entry

Your list might be different than mine and that's totally okay! Honor the spaces that love and loss leave behind by making them beautiful, productive, and full of light. Don't aim to fill them up, aim to make them whole.

3. Don't Give Your Power Away—Share it.

Real talk: We feel powerless because, too often, we give our power away. We blame other people for our problems, we make excuses, we allow ourselves to be taken advantage of, and we gossip and get jealous. Raise your hand if you've ever done any of the above self-sabotaging things. It's okay, nobody's watching.

Being accountable and responsible can seem scary and "too adult," but if we don't embrace these qualities, we let go of our incredible power to heal and help ourselves and others. We miss out on living our most meaningful, fulfilling, and beautiful lives, not just for one dream day, but today, right now. Take control of your power. Make decisions you're proud of. Make mistakes you learn from. Give yourself permission to love, forgive, and grow. Share the things you learn with others and do it with honesty and humility.

Want to try something fun and also maybe bump into some stuff?

Go the darkest room in your house with your phone or a flashlight. Turn off all of the lights, and when you can hardly see anything, sit still and notice how dark it is. Pay attention to the darkness and make a mental note of what it feels like. When you're done, flip that little flashlight on your phone on and try it again. Compare the two experiences. Notice the brightness that your tiny light brings to the room. You didn't have to haul in a grand spotlight, you simply needed your simple light source.

When you turn the power on, your power or your light, you bring your best self to the table. Now notice how much brightness your inner light brings to the dark room. So often we get overwhelmed because we convince ourselves we could never be big enough or important enough to make a difference, or to actually bring hope and love to empty places. But the truth is, look at how much power and light you carry and emit. Look at how you can light up an entire room.

It's never good to give your power away, but sharing it can be beautiful. Do this exercise again with a friend, one who won't get mad at you if she catches her elbow on the bathroom sink. Sit in the dark and then ask her to turn on her light. After her light is on, join her by turning yours on, too. Sharing that goodness, you'll both be standing in the glow. It'll be easier for both of you to be your best selves.

When you find yourself in the dark, take control, find that light, and share it with everyone around you.

4. See the Good. Be the Good.

Pain is a blurry lens. In the months following the loss of my children, I could see nothing but hurt, doubt, and shame; I could feel nothing but brokenness, bleakness, and heartache. Sisters, if this is what you see every time you open your eyes, I understand. I know what this dark world looks like, and I know there are moments when you can hardly bear it. Trust in my promise though: There is so much goodness here, even though right now it is hiding from you.

You have to be brave, and you have to go find it. Start with just one good thing that brings you a moment of relief, hope, or laughter. Write about it if you have to and cling to it, knowing that it's out there waiting for you. The next day or the next week, try to find two good things. Keep going until you lose count. If you simply can't find anything good, you can create it. Do something for someone you love, smile at a stranger, or bring your neighbor a cup of tea. As long you are in this world, precious friend, there is goodness and hope here.

Right before we lost the kids, I had this overpowering thought that if our family were ever to be split up, in order to keep living, I would have to do one kind thing for a stranger every day. I remember shaking the thought from my mind, because it felt disruptive to look into a future I wanted no part in it. However, I wrote this unimaginable future down in my journal because I couldn't shake it. It took me a while to remember that experience after we lost the kids, but one day as I was reading through old entries, I found it. The same conviction I felt the first time the thought entered into my mind came over me again. I'm not perfect at doing at least one kind thing for a stranger each day, but I try. When I do meet this goal, any pain I am carrying magically becomes lighter. God lifts some of my burden from my shoulders for a moment so that I can help someone else carry theirs. God helps me serve.

5: Stop Waiting. Start Right Now.

Tomorrow always seems to look better than today. Maybe we'll have more money. Maybe we'll be skinnier. Maybe we'll fall in love. We spend so much of our lives waiting for the time to be right, for a special occasion or perfect "today," that we forget to live in the moment that has been given to us. We miss out on growth, forward momentum, joy, and opportunity while we're standing around waiting for life to be delivered to us in a neat little package. In the beginning of this book, I gave you permission to be right where you are, to accept it, and to acknowledge it. Now that you have, now that you've honored your pain and looked up at your mountain, you don't have to wait anymore. Go! Chase something! Create something! Build the life you've always wanted. You can stop reading and just go. I won't be mad.

It's easy to say you'll start believing in yourself once you get the dream job, the boob job, or the wedding ring, but there will always be another benchmark. The cycle of waiting to hit just one more milestone, or buying one new status symbol to make ourselves believe we are worth it must end. Sisters, today, you are your own living proof of inherent goodness, strength, and worthiness. We aren't going to get wherever it is we want to go if we don't get moving, so let's go. Today is ours, tomorrow isn't, so let's own this moment. Let me see you stand up and shine.

I'm not a doctor or a therapist, and I don't share my story and my plan because I have all the answers. I share my journey and steps tried and taken because I have hope. I have so much hope for you, and these steps help me find my hope for myself when I've misplaced it. If your journey has left you feeling exhausted, and you want to give up, humor me: try what I'm suggesting just for one week. The worst thing that can happen is you will have spent seven days working on the incredible human that you are. The best that could happen is you start believing in her.

If you want more exercises and a supportive community that will help empower you stand up and shine, we are waiting for you at theshineproject.com/borntoshine.

Chapter Twenty-One:

BORN TO SHINE

A n old note scribbled on a small, torn-out coloring book page sits on my desk as one of my most prized possessions. I found it leaning against the lamp on my nightstand, and it was tucked in so close I'm surprised I didn't miss it. It had been a long day of work, a long day of parenting. It had been a long day of living, really. I was exhausted. The kids had been with us almost three years, and while it had been crazy-bliss for the most part, it had also been just plain crazy, and I had begun to doubt myself. I didn't know if I was being a good employer, a good business owner, and even more importantly, I didn't know if I was being a good wife and mother. I didn't even know if I *could* be good at all of those things at once.

As I sank my head into the pillow, I saw the paper on the table to my left. It was folded into a beautifully crooked boat shape, and I knew immediately where it had come from—S had been working hard on his origami skills. I'd know those little sails anywhere. I picked it up and ran the soft, flimsy paper between my fingertips. Inside, I figured there was probably a Harry Potter-inspired potion or magic spell he wanted to share with me. "I'm tired," I thought. "Whatever it is can probably wait until tomorrow. Besides, everybody knows it's impossible to get armadillo bile and fairy wings past nine o'clock anyway."

I put the sailboat back down, flicked the light off, and rolled over. Within seconds, I rolled back over and turned the light back on. Maybe it was curiosity, maybe it was Mom guilt, but something told me even though S's message *could* wait until tomorrow, the moment to read it was now. I needed to read whatever had been so carefully written and delivered to me. I slowly unfurled every crease, retracing the steps S had taken, and I flattened the paper out between my hands. What I read was tender, and exactly what I needed to hear.

"I love you because you light my way."

I wept. I held the message to my chest and tried to absorb it. Chaos surrounded us, caseworkers were showing up at the door, and we had court dates and bills we could hardly keep up with. Mike and I had never experienced so much uncertainty. I was afraid and felt like I was failing everyone, including myself; but, through this darkness, where self-doubt was eating self-love alive, my little boy still saw me shining. To him, I was still the guardian, the light-bearer, the protector and dispeller of darkness. To him, I was still the unending source of safety and joy. What I saw was a woman losing her battles, but he saw a warrior who was never afraid to fight for him, who bravely led the march, day in and day out. While I was consumed with the shadows in front of me, my son was held safe in the light I was casting behind me. While I was busy "failing," I had become the person I always hoped I could be.

The purpose of this book has not been to tell my story, it has been to get you to take a closer look at your own—the way I so desperately needed to that night when I felt like life was imploding. Is it possible that the reason you don't always see the light you bring to your world is because you are the one who has led the march and ventured boldly into the darkness? Is it possible that *you* are a beacon of hope, a well of love, a blanket of warmth, a light on a dark path, and a leader of all the good things in life to your family, friends, and communities? Is it possible that you are braver and brighter and more of a light than you think you are? It was possible for me.

The gift my son gave me in that little note changed everything. I want to give that same gift to you. Right now, I wish I could be sitting with you speaking these words into you. Sisters, mothers, teachers, daughters, and brokenhearted warriors—you are shining. Whoever you are, whatever you have done, and whatever has been done to you, you belong here. You are beautiful, and you have an inner light that was born to shine. It does not matter how many times you think you've failed, how many times you've been cheated on, or how many times you've cheated. It does not matter if you've made more mistakes than masterpieces, if you don't have much money, or if you don't like the way you look. It doesn't matter how many publishers have passed on your work because it's not good enough (trust me on this one). You are lighting the way for someone just by being here, just by getting up every day and walking into whatever darkness may await. We all face something—you are not alone.

You were born to shine. Nothing less. The darker it gets, the more brilliant and bold your light appears. Do not give up. Continue to stand back up and light the way for others. You are needed here, even if you don't know that you are. I know that sometimes the burden you carry feels like it's too much. Remember though that you don't have to carry it alone. When your arms are too shaky, release and let Him carry it for you. When you can't see the good in this world, create it. When your story seems like it's over, begin new a chapter. Begin right now.

If it has been a bad day—or a bad year—and you haven't been able to step back and take a look at all the people your light has touched, let me be the one to deliver to you again the eight perfect words that changed everything for me: "I love you because you light my way."

Sisters, this is your time. You were made for this. You were made for it all. You were born to shine.

This page belongs to you. Begin a new chapter. Start right now. Write that letter to yourself that gives you all the courage and permission to shine again.

Love, Ashley.

ACKNOWLEDGEMENTS

Thank you, to my Shine Project community. You were with me when I was stamping necklaces out of that old cockroach infested condo, you've cheered me on when I've launched new businesses, you've pinned my hair tutorials and outfits on the internet, you've sent me thousands of messages and emails telling me you're rooting me on and praying for my family. You tell me that you love wearing The Shine Project jewelry and clothing. You are the ultimate cheerleaders a girl could ask for, and because of you, so much has been brought to life. We've done some amazing things together, and I can't wait to continue on this journey through life with you!

Thank you to Bryan Norman, who challenged me to put my writing out into the world. I will never forget sitting across from you while I was eating pepperoni pizza, listening to you tell me you believed in me. You did what only a great literary agent and human being would do, you championed me even when plans changed. I'm grateful for the confidence you helped build in me to make this dream come true.

I owe the most heartfelt thank you to Shannon, who encouraged these words in the most tender, powerful way, and used all the

185

magic pixie dust I'm certain she keeps in her pocket to make this project fly. You, sister, are a treasure.

I am grateful for the team at Morgan James, for helping bring to life this project. David, you helped change the trajectory of this book, and I'm grateful that you put your expertise and knowledge behind projects like mine.

A lot goes on behind the scenes in writing and running businesses. It's what goes on behind the scenes that is the most important. Thank you to my team at The Shine Project and Shop Ashley LeMieux for keeping the little engine that could running. You are all team players who have jumped onto the crazy train with me to take the wildest rides. It took time to find each one of you, and your work and efforts are never lost on me.

Brooke, I know you are reading this, because I know you always read every word. You've been my biggest cheerleader from the time I pushed you down when we were little to steal your popsicles, to when I would lock you out of my room so you couldn't play with "us big girls" in junior high, to when you knew I would be a great mother to my children before I did. You are my best friend, my most trusted confidant, and my truest Sisto.

To my family, I am grateful that I get to go through life with you. Thanks for always being in the front row, telling me I can do anything I set my mind to, no matter how hard it gets. Sunday dinners are my biggest treasure.

Thank you to my children who made me a mother, S and Z. I often wonder how out of all the billions of people in the world, life orchestrated perfectly to allow us to be together for a time. I know our shared path was not born by chance or accident. In allowing me to be your mother, God gave me the greatest privilege of my life. I pray for the day when I get to squeeze you again. Love knows no time limits, and I want you to always know that my love for you is constant and enduring.

Last, and most definitely not least, thank you to my husband, Mike LeMieux, who has walked through life with me side-by-side. Mike, you hold my hand when I need it, and you let me fly when I'm ready. You seeing me changed me.

ABOUT THE AUTHOR

Ashley LeMieux is an author, sought-after public speaker, and wildly successful lifestyle influencer. She's the founder of the online community The Shine Project, where she is a cheerleader for women and creates resources and tools that have ignited a path of clarity and fulfillment for hundreds of thousands of women around the world. Through her fashion and lifestyle brand, Shop Ashley LeMieux, she empowers "Women Who Do" to show up confidently and courageously to their lives. She believes that you can turn your pain into your power.

Connect with her on Instagram @AshleyKLeMieux.
Find more resources to empower your life at
theshineproject.com/borntoshine.
Discover her clothing line at ashleylemieux.com.